SANCTIFICATION:
AN ALLIANCE
DISTINCTIVE

SANCTIFICATION: AN ALLIANCE DISTINCTIVE

by
Samuel J. Stoesz

Christian Publications

CAMP HILL, PENNSYLVANIA

Christian Publications
3825 Hartzdale Drive, Camp Hill, PA 17011

The mark of ✝ *vibrant faith*

ISBN: 0-87509-493-7
LOC Catalog Card Number: 92-70289
© 1992 by Christian Publications
All rights reserved
Printed in the United States of America

92 93 94 95 96   5 4 3 2 1

Contents

ACKNOWLEDGMENTS

It is difficult to give adequate recognition to those who have contributed to the preparation of this book. First, it was Dr. Richard W. Bailey, vice president of Church Ministries who initially suggested the need for an historically grounded approach to a doctrine so formative to The Christian and Missionary Alliance. His encouragement and confidence was largely responsible for this writing.

Secondly, I am deeply indebted:

For the editorial assistance of Dr. Maurice Irvin, editor of *Alliance Life*. His forthright comments, logical questions and expert editorial assistance despite his many other responsibilities were extremely critical to the final draft.

To the readers of the manuscript—Dr. L.L. King, Dr. Arnold Cook, Dr. Donald Wiggins, Rev. Robert L. Nicklaus and Dr. Harold P. Shelly—whose observations made important contributions. Also to Mrs. Lynn Munson, who so patiently enabled a computer novice in the initial stages.

The freedom given to the author's interpretive expression was so unrestricted and so totally uncensored that responsibility for what is written is understood to rest with the author. The areas of question in the minds of critical readers are open for discussion and further investigation. The motivation behind this book is to facilitate understanding and to cultivate a deeper conviction of a legacy most crucial to Alliance heritage.

FOREWORD

During the past decade numerous books on the charismatic revival and the "signs and wonders" movement have led multitudes to a peak of excitement and expectancy. All too often readers have been left disillusioned, disappointed and unchanged; Christ's kingdom has not been advanced, nor has the Church found desperately needed spiritual renewal. Perhaps this failure is due to inadequate theology which is incapable of bringing the centrality of Christ into clear focus.

A.B. Simpson was a man who interpreted the whole Bible in Christological truth: "Christ was everything and everything was in Christ." Neither power, signs, nor gifts were his focus, but rather Christ Himself revealed through holy Scripture.

Dr. Samuel J. Stoesz presents here an historical treatise of Simpson's understanding of Christology. He has carefully researched the writings and teachings of Simpson to discover the historical development of the truth, "Christ our Sanctifier."

The author clearly delineates the difference between Simpson's teaching about sanctification and those views of the Wesleyan, Keswick (dispensationalist), Pentecostal and Charismatic movements. Simpson asserts that Christ alone is our sanctification and Christ alone is our authority for service. The Holy Spirit speaks not of Himself but reveals the person of Christ for purity of life and power for service through union in Christ.

This book is for Christian leaders and workers in the evangelical community, and will be specially welcomed by those serving in The Christian and Missionary Alliance. Stoesz so ably says:

> *Our day of sudden change needs both theology and an historical perspective. Where an historical understanding is least real,*

the theological understanding is most empty. Since the New Testament Church has been nurtured by the word of Christ and the Holy Spirit has taught faithful members, a history of theology must be taken seriously as a heritage left to us for instruction. If we do not know where we have come from, we do not know where we are or where we are going.

Stoesz is well qualified to write this treatise, having served as a pastor and professor of theology in The Christian and Missionary Alliance for over 40 years. He is a student of Alliance history and was a major contributor to *All for Jesus*, the centennial history of The Christian and Missionary Alliance. He has authored several other books, including the well-known publication *Understanding My Church.*

It is my prayer that this volume will enable Christian leaders to understand more fully and articulate more adequately the glorious truth of Christ our Sanctifier.

Richard Weber Bailey
Vice President for Church Ministries
The Christian and Missionary Alliance

1
The Urgent Appeal

A popular theologian of our day has called our times a "cut-flower civilization." Elton Trueblood has written: "The terrible danger of our time consists in the fact that ours is a cut-flower civilization. Beautiful as cut flowers may be, and much as we may use our ingenuity to keep them looking fresh for a while, they will eventually die, and they die because they are severed from their sustaining roots. We are trying to maintain the dignity of the individual apart from the deep faith that every man is made in God's image and is therefore precious in God's eyes."[1]

Similarly, the Alliance is in danger of becoming a cut-flower religious movement. The doctrine of sanctification has a special relevance to the identity of The Christian and Missionary Alliance. No emphasis had a greater influence on its founding. It shaped its development and was a prime element in the selection of its priorities. But sanctification seems to have lost its significance, and unless the vital connection to its roots is restored, it may well die. The virgin power of a beginning is seldom sustained because those who come into a movement later, tend to assume its continuance without cultivation of its roots.

It is disconcerting to contemplate the results if certain

underlying principles were suddenly eliminated from familiar institutions. For example, those who originally framed the constitution of the United States stated in the preamble that they held certain truths to be self-evident; that all men are created equal and are endowed with certain inalienable rights for life, liberty and the pursuit of happiness. Suppose these principles were ignored. What difference would this make to American liberty and democracy? To the American judicial system? Similarly, to neglect what has been a founding conviction of the Alliance movement, what has shaped and molded its development, also has dire implications.

The Current Need for Holiness

Granted, today holiness is not a major concern among believers. Whereas this issue was considered essential in 1887, when the C&MA was founded, today it seems so retired into recess that evangelical believers are almost unaware of any specific doctrine of holiness.

Recent attempts to revive interest in the doctrine of sanctification are revealing. Two books on "five views of sanctification" have recently been published, both of which feature the presentation of particular views followed by interacting dialogues.[2] Such a smorgasbord attempt would not have appeared in 1887 when roots of conviction ran deep and theological traditions were strong. But the need for holiness has surfaced in the 1990s with an unusual urgency.

Men of high profile in television, notably Jim Bakker and Jimmy Swaggart, have drastically besmirched the gospel with scandals of such scope and enormity that they have caught the attention and scorn not only of believers but of unbelievers around the world. The National American Securities Administration in Washington, D.C., recently published a list of so-called Christian organizations who have bilked sincere people of many millions of dollars.[3] The occurrence of divorce among Christian leaders has become distressingly common. While many factors contribute to the situation, the modern mindset is particularly significant.

Since World War II, existentialism with its subjective and relative approach to reality has permeated our culture. Churches tend to drift with the thinking of the age. Because truth is not considered absolute, convictions and commitments become tentative and subject to change. The need for decisive obedience and love for truth as it is in Christ runs counter to the modern way of thinking. Loyalties become temporary and historical tradition almost useless.

Based on the assumption of scientific probability, modern existentialism views man as an alien and an accident in the cosmos; man exists without purpose. With organic evolution as a major premise, existentialism ignores God's sovereignty over creation and final judgment. Thus, truth is undermined and mere subjectivism tends to prevail. "What feels good must be right" has become an accepted philosophy not only by the drug culture but by religious culture. A spiritual "high" may be substituted for a relationship with God without considering the cross and its moral implications.

The result of secular influence is that immorality is tolerated even in so-called evangelical circles. Though it may appear as a cliché, only a genuine revival of biblical holiness rooted in historical theology and proclaimed by anointed preaching can ultimately effect the change so desperately needed.

Several evangelical leaders are raising cries of alarm. J.I. Packer of Regent College in Canada estimates that since the Reformation, Protestant Christians have probably never been more unsure, tentative and confused as to what they should believe or do. Billy Graham, at a recent academic convocation, expressed the concern that American Christianity has lost sight of the fact that some things are always right and that some things are always wrong, that ultimately our reference point has been lost.[4]

A conference of 350 evangelical leaders met in May of 1989 to consider the doctrinal stance of the National Association of Evangelicals because "its cognitive content and its life ethic had both suffered to the point that the vitality and even survival of the movement may be questioned." At this conference, evangelical spokesman Carl F.H. Henry stated that the evangelicals' sense of their own identity and purpose as well as their public image had never been more murky and maligned.[5]

A deep concern for genuine holiness of life and character appears to be rising. But again, only a genuine revival of biblical holiness rooted in historical theology and proclaimed by anointed preaching can ultimately effect the change so desperately needed.

In my denomination, The Christian and Missionary Alliance, this is a matter of special concern because the vitality of this movement and its ability to impact the world has depended upon an emphasis on sanctification.

The Importance of Sanctification in the Alliance

A.B. Simpson, the founder of the C&MA believed that both the support system and the missionary force deployed by the Alliance needed to be united in a faith in Christ's fullness. He firmly resisted a generalist approach to the missionary mandate and cultivated only those who believed in Christ as Sanctifier and relied upon His sufficiency for life and service.

In 1900, Simpson wrote *The Story of The Christian and Missionary Alliance,* and in the opening paragraph stated that the movement had been founded:

> *for the purpose of uniting in Christian fellowship and testimony,*
> *in a purely fraternal alliance, the large number of consecrated*
> *Christians in the various evangelical churches, who believed*

*in the Lord Jesus as Savior, Sanctifier, Healer and coming
Lord, and also uniting their effort in the special aggressive
work of world-wide evangelization. . . . Within the past quarter
of a century especially, God had been calling large numbers of His
people into a deeper life, and Christ has been revealing Himself,
personally, to them as a complete Savior and uniting Himself to
them through the Holy Ghost as an indwelling presence and all-
sufficient Sanctifier . . .*[6]

According to Simpson, the distinctive that initially united
people in the Alliance was not evangelism or missions per se
but their experience of Christ in sanctifying power. World
evangelism was not considered the cause but the effect of
knowing Christ in His fullness. The Christ of all authority
over the universe (Matthew 28:18-20; Acts 1:8) was considered enthroned and enfleshed in God's people. Through His
fullness by the Spirit a missionary enterprise was not only
possible but inherent to the obedience of God's people.

The Contemporary Theological Challenge

Since its founding and early development, the Alliance
"ship of state" has undergone much change both in its structure and in its operation. To simply hark back to "the good old
branch and tabernacle days" when the Alliance still func-
tioned as an interdenominational missionary society will not
work in our present situation. The Alliance has become a
denomination with corporate responsibility and accountability.

Though Simpson's methods of work were effective, some
aspects no longer meet the demands of our day nor the needs
of our culture. New questions, changes in development and
challenges of perspective demand critical probing and investigation. This does not mean that the original message and
methods were unsound; it simply means that Alliance people

must understand the biblical principles that will keep them in the will and calling of God for our times.

While knowledgeable members or adherents of the Alliance may differ in certain details of interpretation regarding its history, particularly with respect to the development of the Alliance position on sanctification, the need for constructive investigation is nevertheless urgent. As someone has so aptly observed: "If our distinctive emphasis on the centrality of Christ in personal faith and missions is an outdated cliché, the Alliance has only a limited contribution to make to the evangelical community."[7]

Historically, the message and mission of the Alliance in particular made it a significant member of the evangelical community. It must continue to be a force for Christ in the world in order to fulfill its calling.

The Critical Need for Balance

A comprehensive view of development in the history of the Alliance reveals how theology and practice are affected by prevailing secular thought. Particularly, it reveals the need for balance between theology and practice.

Two major shifts in the philosophy of American culture have effected the evangelical movement as it emerged out of the revival of 1857-58. This revival was characterized by public response to gospel preaching and the urgent need for world evangelization in view of Christ's coming again. D.L. Moody and A.B. Simpson were typical representatives of this evangelical movement before the turn of century.

The first shift in American secular thought came as the 19th century closed. Prior to 1900, a Judeo-Christian value system permeated North American culture. This was evidenced in the education of youth. From the founding of Harvard in 1636 and to the post-Civil War period that followed, some 300 colleges were begun by American churches to instruct youth in the Christian faith. However, the winds of change began to blow from Europe and particularly from the German universities. A scientific approach to learning and organizing knowledge became known as the age of enlightenment.

The philosophy behind this approach was logical positivism which held that little can be known with certainty and that true knowledge is limited to experimentation and organized sense perception. Man was the master of his own fate and the measure of all things with an infinite potential to improve himself. Biblical criticism and anti-supernaturalism became popularly known as liberalism. Though this was countered by a movement in evangelicalism called fundamentalism, it still had a notorious effect. The idea, "if it works it must be right," suited the industrial revolution of the late 19th century and in turn influenced the evangelical church.

Church and mission historians observe that the great evangelical missionary thrust as spearheaded by The Student Volunteer movement of the late 19th and early 20th century, peaked at the Edinburgh International Missionary Conference in 1910 because of theological defection and an over-balanced emphasis on social concern. A popular slogan at this conference was "Service unites, doctrine divides"; consequently doctrine was minimized or overlooked and the practical was given prominence.

Though the Alliance, organized in 1887, was not specifically threatened by liberalism nor caught up in fundamentalism, its doctrinal stance was not honed or strengthened as the founder and his immediate colleagues passed from the scene of action. A revealing anecdote concerning H.M. Shuman who became Alliance president in 1926, illustrates this neglect. He enjoyed recounting how his friend, G. Verner Brown, had heard so much about sanctification he became confused. Convinced of his need for a deeper experience of God's grace, Brown prayed, "Lord, give me sanctification as you understand it." With obvious personal satisfaction, Dr. Shuman concluded, "That solved the problem for him as far as heart experience was concerned."[8]

This pragmatic solution is a tragic commentary on leaders of the Alliance since Brown served as home secretary and Shuman as president. Such an approach may suffice when a theological foundation has been laid though not fully understood by the seeker, but is wholly inadequate for leadership. In the 20s and 30s an imbalance between theology and practice was freely tolerated. Free enterprise agencies and institutions multiplied to meet particular needs with little discipline in doctrine or accountability. This climate, in measure, affected The Christian and Missionary Alliance.

However, the cultural climate out of which Simpson's convictions of the doctrine of sanctification developed was different. Both of Simpson's parents came from Scotland as Covenanters. His father was a leading elder in the Presbyterian church where doctrinal discipline was of major importance. Simpson memorized the Shorter Catechism by age 12. In his home were books on sanctification by Puritan writers: Richard Baxter's *Saint's Rest*; Philip Doddridge's *Rise and Progress of Religion in the Soul*, and Walter Marshall's *The Gospel Mystery of Sanctification*. Herbert F. Stevenson in *Keswick's Authentic Voice* observes that Marshall's book "contains all that Keswick later re-minted in present-day language."[9]

There were no radios, televisions or even newspapers in the farm home. By age 14 Simpson recorded this solemn covenant:

I have now, O Lord, as Thou hast said in Thy Word, Covenanted with Thee, not for worldly honors or fame but for everlasting life, and I know that Thou art true and shalt never break Thy holy Word. Give to me now all the blessings of the New Covenant and especially the Holy Spirit in great abundance, which is the earnest of my inheritance until the redemption of the purchased possession. May a double portion of Thy Spirit rest upon me, and then I shall go and proclaim to transgressors Thy ways and Thy laws to the people. Sanctify me wholly and make me fit for heaven. Give me all spiritual blessing in heavenly places in Christ Jesus.[10]

It would appear that Simpson experienced sanctification at an early age, but neither the doctrine nor the experience came into focus until 17 years later.

The Church of Scotland had gone through a disruption in 1843, and The Free Church (Presbyterian) was organized under the leadership of Thomas Chalmers. The Free Church was the parent church of Knox College, Toronto, from which Simpson graduated in 1864. When Simpson attended, Knox College was still staffed by professors from Scotland who believed that a good theological education depended on an ability to understand and interpret the Scriptures in their original languages. Michael Willis, Simpson's theology teacher, covered "the Covenant of Redemption—the person and offices of Christ—the atonement (orthodox and middle schemes)—impetration and application of spiritual benefits— Union to Christ—Faith (Pelagian, Semipelagian, Neonomian, Antinomian, views refuted)."[11]

Simpson's view of the atonement shows strong resemblance to that of George Smeaton, a Free Church theologian who authored two classical works on the subject in 1868 and 1870.[12] His Christology and world view seem derived from a contemporary Free Church theologian, James Orr.[13] Heavy underlinings and marginal comments in his copies of Thomas Goodwin's works, a Puritan writer and theologian, suggest that Simpson's view of a crisis of the deeper life found its roots there. Goodwin emphasized both the need for conversion and the need for full assurance of salvation that resembled Simpson's emphasis on the deeper life.

When Simpson's understanding of sanctification coalesced into firm conviction and a transforming experience in 1874, he was reading W.E. Boardman's *The Higher Christian Life*. Boardman, like Simpson, was nourished in the same theological framework. Simpson did not have an experience he substantiated with selected proof-texts and a superficial theology, but one undergirded by a theology rooted in rich soil he had cultivated during all his formative years.

The diminished emphasis upon theology that characterized the early 1900s affected the C&MA, though its principal views were founded on Simpson's theological understanding. For Simpson, theology came first and the practical flowed from it, whereas the practical often became more important than the theological as the Alliance and evangelicalism as a whole developed in the 20th century.

A second shift of philosophy in American culture came after World War II. Relativity now gripped the popular mind and man was left without a mission control center. Man's feeling experiences became punctuated with a craze for hard rock music, a quest for horror thrills and addiction to drugs. Liberalism gave way to neo-orthodoxy with its faith in myth and its experience in paradox.

But in spite of this extreme trend in modern culture toward subjective experience unbalanced from objective truth and reality, inner experience is needed to know truth in personal living even though experience is not truth by itself. Theologically, there is a balance between objective revelation and subjective experience that is so needed today. God has given man objective revelation through nature (Romans 1:18-20). He has particularly given man objective revelation through His Word which includes Christ's historical incarnation in a world distorted by sin (Hebrews 1:1-3). However, unless the Holy Spirit applies the Word and brings Christ to the heart, truth will remain dormant and ineffective even when a man's theology appears to be orthodox.

The Pharisees were meticulous in their reverence for the Scriptures and the scribes were scrupulous copiers to guard its jots and tittles, yet Jesus said: "You diligently study the Scriptures because you think that by them you possess eternal life. These are the Scriptures that testify about me, yet you refuse to come to me to have life" (John 5:39-40).

Christ the truth and the life must be realized as the focus of Scripture. Both the Scriptures and the risen life of Christ by the Holy Spirit are essential. On the other hand, those who consciously or unconsciously make experience autonomous, eventually put an end to final authority and inevitably drift with the relativistic modern tide into a moral morass.

Evangelicalism today is frequently divided between a battle for the Bible and a battle for the Holy Spirit. That Christ Himself represents a balance for both has been the message of The Christian and Missionary Alliance. When our Lord was here upon earth, He taught His disciples that the Spirit's ministry would be to focus the believers' faith on Himself, Jesus Christ, the Savior of the world. He alone represents both objective and subjective authority. This characterized the emphasis of the Alliance.

In neglect of doctrine, the Alliance often seems to be caught in a tension of uncertainty. On the one hand, the Reformation doctrine of *Sola Scriptura* is considered essential. On the other hand, the subjectivistic religious movements of our day and their apparent success pull her in another direction. But both the objective revelation and subjective experience were originally seen as united in Christ. The great danger is failure to see that the objective precedes the subjective if balance is to be realized.

It is believed that the meaning and significance of "Christ Himself and His fullness" that so strongly characterized the Alliance in its beginnings, is basic to Alliance identity for

- How?

today. Yet, this has eroded and weakened with time. This is because theology is neglected while the practical and the subjective displace doctrine in order and significance.

The Personal and Corporate Responsibility

Faithfulness to a divine calling and mission is essential to every church or denomination's right to exist. In essence, that is the message of Christ to the seven churches in the book of Revelation, chapters 2 and 3. "He who has an ear, let him hear what the Spirit says to the churches" is repeated to each of the seven churches. Jesus Christ, the Head of the churches, demanded discipline in the churches' message and mission.

The main threat to the seven churches was not what was happening from without, even though we know severe persecutions and corrupt philosophies were impacting the churches. The messages addressed what was happening from within. Each church was given certain warnings as well as certain commendations from its record of performance. The assumption throughout is that God has founded each church, has given it His Word, and that the Holy Spirit is bearing witness to truth as it is in Christ among the faithful. The church is thus established as "the pillar and ground of truth" (1 Timothy 3:15) to withstand the forces of evil, both from within and from without.

To the church of Thyatira, Christ's command concluded: "Only hold on to what you have until I come. To him who overcomes and does my will to the end, I will give authority over the nations . . . just as I have received authority from my Father" (Revelation 2:25-27). The church is recognized as God's agency through which doctrinal or spiritual discipline and mission is to be accomplished, but the transmission of the authority of Christ depends upon a union with Christ which His substitutionary work established.

To the church at Ephesus the message was: "Remember the height from which you have fallen! Repent and do the things you did at first" (Revelation 2:5). To remember Alliance history particularly regarding its emphasis on the deeper life is a formidable challenge. Especially is this true because the Alliance was "an interdenominational missionary society emphasizing the deeper Christian life and missions." It had no constitutional statement of doctrine until 1965. Yet, as its history reveals, the early branch functions fostered a membership committed to a particular message and mission, and indigenous churches were planted to represent the same message and mission.

The scriptural appeal for the churches "to hold on to what you have" cannot be dismissed by this generation of Alliance people. Does The Christian and Missionary Alliance believe that our fellowship of faith can be defined in a unified way? Dare we separate our mission from our original message? If we do not, the appeal "to hold on to what you have" is urgent.

FOOTNOTES

[1] James R. Newby, *Elton Trueblood, Believer, Teacher, and Friend,* (San Francisco: Harper & Row, Publishers, 1990), p. 67.

[2] *Five Views on Sanctification,* (Grand Rapids: Zondervan Pub. Co. 1987). This book represented: the Wesleyan perspective by Melvin E. Dieter; the Reformed by Anthony A. Hoekema; the Keswick by J. Robertson McQuilkin; the Pentecostal by Stanley M. Horton and the Augustinian-Dispensational by John F. Walvoord. *Christian Spirituality, Five Views of Sanctification,* edited by Donald L. Alexander. (Downers Grove: InterVarsity Press, 1988). The views represented are: the Lutheran by Gerhard O. Forde; the Reformed by Sinclair W. Wood; the Wesleyan by Laurence W. Wood; the Pentecostal

by Russell P. Spittler and the Contemplative by E. Glenn Hinson.

3 Letter published by the North American Securities Administration, Inc., 555 New Jersey Avenue, N.W. Suite 750. Washington, D.C., September, 1989.

4 "What Does It Mean to Be Evangelical?" *Christianity Today*, June 16, 1989, News, pp. 60, 63.

5 Ibid.

6 A.B. Simpson, *The Story of the Christian and Missionary Alliance*, (New York: Alliance Press, 1900), p. 3.

7 From a memo to Richard Bailey, James Davey by Robert T. Niklaus, June 24, 1987.

8 Robert T. Niklaus, John S. Sawin, Samuel J. Stoesz, *All For Jesus*, (Camp Hill, PA: Christian Publications, Inc., 1986), p. 165.

9 Herbert F. Stevenson (ed.), *Keswick's Authentic Voice*, (Grand Rapids: Zondervan, 1959), Introduction.

10 A.E. Thompson, *A.B. Simpson, His Life and Work*, (Harrisburg: Christian Publications, Inc., 1960), p. 22.

11 Richard W. Vaudry, "Theology and education in early Victorian Canada: Knox College Toronto, 1844-61," *Studies in Religion*, Fall/'87, p. 443.

12 George Smeaton, *The Doctrine of the Atonement as taught by Christ Himself*, (Edinburgh: T & T. Clark, 1871) and *The Doctrine of the Atonement as taught by the Apostles*, (Edinburgh: T & T Clark, 1870). Wilbur M. Smith writes a biographical sketch in the first volume listed and says: "The two most exhaustive, satisfying studies of New Testament passages bearing upon the pre-eminently-sacred subject of the death of our Lord Jesus Christ."

13 James Orr, *A Christian View of God and the World*, (Edinburg: Andrew Elliot, 5th ed., 1893). Orr (1844-1913), as a leading United Free Church Presbyterian of Scotland, had significant influence in North America.

2
The Roots

Perhaps no evangelical movement that sprang up previous to the 20th century has sustained a more singular identity with its founder than has The Christian and Missionary Alliance. A.W. Tozer reflected on this when he wrote:

> *His society is himself grown large. It is the child of his heart, and it resembles its father as all good children should. The same humility is seen in it to this day, the same distrust of the flesh, the same preoccupation with the person of Christ.*[1]

The Alliance has frequently been characterized as a deeper life and missionary movement. Simpson described his view on sanctification with the expressions "the fullness of Jesus" or "the all-sufficiency of Christ" or simply, "Christ Himself."

However, he was not the originator of such an emphasis. The nomenclature and emphasis began with W.E. Boardman and the movement that resulted from the book he published in 1859 under the title, *The Higher Christian Life*. It was embedded in the early Keswick movement in the late 1870s among such men as Andrew Murray, J. Wilbur Chapman, A.J. Gordon, G. Campbell Morgan, J. Hudson Taylor, F.B. Meyer and A.T. Pierson, but the emphasis faded as the Keswick movement distanced itself from the higher Christian life movement, its filial forerunner.

No one comes to his faith *de novo*, no one can claim originality or independence for his convictions. There is always a context from which strands of truth come to focus and into life-dynamics. This was the case with Albert Simpson.

Threads of Influence

In the spring of 1874, while pastoring Chestnut Street Presbyterian Church in Louisville, Kentucky, Simpson had a life-changing experience. This came about while he was confronting difficult circumstances moving from Canada to Louisville.

Like the Baptists and Methodists, the Presbyterians were split north and south when the Civil War ended in 1865. Louisville was on the Mason-Dixon line, the border between north and south. The estimated cost of the Civil War was one million lives and 10 billion in gold value and was the most divisive and heart-rending experience in American history. As a pastor, Simpson found himself stymied in the muck of hatred, prejudice and wounded spirits which only a genuine revival would remedy.

The religious awakening in England under D.L. Moody's ministry in 1872-73 stirred Simpson's vision. Moody testified to an infilling with the Holy Spirit in 1871 that had transformed his ministry. Moody's preaching, however, consisted mainly of a call to salvation presented as a "one-shot, do or die, this is it proposition." He preached that Christ could deliver from all sin and the desire for it through the new birth and the enabling of the Holy Spirit.[2]

Toward the end of Moody's campaign in England, two men, W.E. Boardman and R. Pearsall Smith visited England from America. Boardman's book *The Higher Christian Life*, published in America in 1859, had been distributed widely by several publishers in England. Smith, a wealthy glassmaker from Philadelphia and a lay minister, was a friend of Board-man. His business brought him into contact with influential church ministers in England. Interest in holiness and its relation to Moody's evangelism captured the attention of the church leaders in England. Boardman and Smith represented a message of holiness well known in America but distinct from the holiness message espoused by the National Holiness Association of Methodist origin.[3]

Boardman had made a business trip to England in 1869. Though unplanned and unpublicized, meetings with unusual response evolved as a result of the interest aroused by his book. Returning to America, Boardman was persuaded from his experience in England to form an association for holding union, holiness conventions in 1870. Meetings, with unusual response, were held in Newark, Philadelphia, Wilmington, New York, Brooklyn, Williamsburg, Syracuse, Providence, Boston and numerous other places on the eastern seaboard as well as in the larger cities of Ohio and Indiana.

Boardman's conventions had a similarity to the National Holiness meetings in that holiness was stressed, but they were uniquely different in message and persuasion. Historically they had no association. The large crowds and overwhelming response so taxed Boardman's health at age 65 that he was forced to seek relief from the mineral waters in Ems, Germany. Meanwhile, Smith, a protégé of Boardman for 30 years,[4] had come to England in 1873 and begun holding meetings on "the higher Christian life." He requested that Boardman, now at Ems, Germany, join him.

In England, a member of the English Parliament from Bristol, named Samuel Morely, sponsored breakfast meetings for ministers featuring Smith and Boardman, though Boardman was still restricted by poor health. It is said that about 2,400 ministers from England, France, Belgium, Norway, Sweden, Holland, Switzerland and Germany attended these break-

fasts. In 1874, at the time of Simpson's deeper-life experience, about 1,000 ministers attended an Oxford Convention on
"the higher Christian life."[5] Simpson had obtained a copy of
The Higher Christian Life but apparently neglected to read it.
Searching for an answer to the factious situation in
Louisville, Simpson decided to attend a Christian Worker's conference sponsored by the Moody Evangelistic Association in
Chicago. He arrived about six p.m. A preconference testimonial service was being held that Simpson rushed to attend.

Presently, a "dear brother" rose and in a broken, sobbing
voice said: "Friends, I came here to get something from the
meeting; but God took me out alone with Him, and I have had
such a sight of Jesus that I will never need anybody or anything
again." Simpson recounts that he was so smitten in his heart, he
did not stay for the conference, but instead took the next
train home.

Back in Louisville in his study, he locked the door and
determined to wait on God. During his vigil he spied "an old
musty book," *The Higher Christian Life*, and began to read.
Later, during a special 50th anniversary of his ordination
sponsored by the Knox Presbyterian Church, his first pastorate, Simpson commented on the impact of Boardman's
book upon him.

Simpson's Crisis Experience

Simpson began his address to his former congregation
with these words: "An occasion so unique as this may justify a
personal testimony, and the opening up of the holiest and most
sacred confidence of one's Christian life."[6] He then recounted
that as a young man of 21 years, God had been pleased to give
him a loyal and united congregation and a successful ministry
beyond anything he had a right to expect. However, even
after nine years, when he moved to Louisville, he had not

yet learned truths of the deeper life. Very thoroughly, patiently and inexorably, God had taught him his own nothingness. When seeking counsel from an old, experienced friend, he was told: "All you need in order to bring you this blessing you are seeking, and to make your life a power for God is to be annihilated." The advice had shocked him, but he began to understand the text "I am not sufficient to think anything of myself" (paraphrase of 2 Corinthians 3:5).

As he continued to address the people at Knox Church, Simpson explained how God taught him the all-sufficiency of Christ. He would never forget the morning in his study when he happened upon *The Higher Christian Life*. In the past he had struggled long and hard with his intense nature, his strong self-will and peculiar temptations. He had often attempted to speak to his people about the deeper things of the Spirit, "but there was a hollow ring and his heart was breaking to know the Lord Jesus as a living bright reality." But as he poured over the little volume by Boardman, he saw new light. Speaking of this experience in the third person, Simpson described it in these words:

> *The Lord Jesus revealed Himself as a living and all-sufficient presence, and he learned for the first time that Christ had not saved us from future peril and left us to fight the battle of life as best we could, but He who had justified us was waiting to sanctify us, to enter into our spirit and substitute His strength, His holiness, His joy, His love, His faith, His power, for all our worthlessness, and make it an actual and living fact, "I will dwell in you and walk in you." Across the threshold of his spirit there passed a Being as real as the Christ who came to John on Patmos, and from that moment a new secret has been the charm, and glory, and strength of his life and testimony.[7]*

Simpson claimed in his testimony that this experience had not only unfolded the secret of spiritual victory but the revelation had also become the source of his mental and physical strength according to the biblical promise: "God is able to make all grace abound to you, so that in all things at all times, having all that you need, you will abound in every good work" (2 Corinthians 9:8). But the most wonderful aspect of this revelation of Christ was in relation to answered prayer. Simpson said, "This great secret opens heaven and puts in our hand a check book which only needs the endorsement of faith to give us fellowship with all the wealth of God's providence and grace."

As Simpson continued his address at Knox, he explained how faith in Christ's fullness became a challenge for the completion of world evangelization and the coming again of Jesus Christ. In fact, he believed a new renaissance of church history was unfolding in the opening of the 20th century to which he was now a participant because of his encounter with Christ and the power of His Spirit.

Effects upon Simpson's Ministry

In his sermon at Knox Church Simpson did not elaborate upon the results of the encounter he described as "the holiest and most sacred confidences of his life." However, historical highlights of his ministry from 1874 to the opening of the 20th century reveal the significance of this encounter to his life and ministry of which he testified.

Shortly after this crisis experience in 1874, Simpson approached the Louisville ministerium about the need for united prayer and suggested that the churches of the city unitedly sponsor the Major Whittle and P.P. Bliss team of the Moody Evangelistic Association. His fellow pastors agreed and joint prayer meetings were rotated among the churches with encouraging response. Additionally, the Whittle/Bliss team was engaged.

Whittle, like Moody, preached for decisions at an altar. His messages, however, had a stronger emphasis on the filling of the Holy Spirit. He stressed that with a true and full commitment at salvation the Holy Spirit was received but that an infilling of the Holy Spirit suppressed the carnal nature and gave enabling power for service. Boardman and the higher Christian life movement, however, focused on a faith-union with Christ Himself as Sanctifier, whose power and authority was realized by an infilling of the Holy Spirit. To the average person this focus on the centrality of Christ Himself was mostly unrecognized, but it had significant implications.

The "higher life" or "deeper life" emphasis of holiness in Boardman and Simpson was not an eradication of sin and the sin nature as the National Holiness Movement held. Rather, it represented the need to realize the reality of a believer's fallen nature and nothingness in himself and in self-relinquishment to appropriate the fullness of Christ's authority and power in the person and work of the Holy Spirit. Whether such an experience took place at conversion or later was not important, but the critical need was to realize Christ's fullness and sufficiency as a living Sanctifier.[8]

At the time of the Whittle/Bliss meetings in Louisville, there is no hint of any differences between Whittle and Simpson. Rather, the effect of the services made evangelism a vital part of Simpson's ministry. Memoirs of the meetings by P.P. Bliss, the song-leading team member, indicate that 2,500 to 3,000 attended each service with three and four meetings being held in one day. About 5,000 were converted.

After the Whittle/Bliss meetings closed, Simpson continued Sunday night evangelistic meetings in a neutral auditorium. Shortly afterward, Broadway Tabernacle was built by Chestnut Street Church to accommodate 2,000 people without the traditional pew rent. Simpson did not conduct special holiness meetings; his preaching called sinners to faith in Christ and believers to sanctifying grace through Christ's fullness and sufficiency by the Holy Spirit. This was all a part of the same gospel.

Climbing a Steep Ascent

Outwardly, Simpson seemed to have reached a satisfying plateau of ministry in Louisville, but not so. He was still climbing a steep ascent. His heart was directed toward world evangelism. The debt incurred in building Broadway Tabernacle (with expensive features not anticipated) deeply disturbed him. He dreamed of a missionary magazine that would challenge churches cross-denominationally and of a cosmopolitan church where evangelism and missions would be supported by consecrated and Spirit-filled believers.

When Simpson received a call from 13th Street Presbyterian in New York City, he saw an opportunity to fulfill his dreams. New York City was an American melting pot where thousands of European immigrants were arriving each year. This was a ready-made mission field that beckoned him.

All went well for Simpson as pastor for some time. New members were added and attendance increased, and the missionary magazine was launched with success. But soon tensions began to surface. When they interviewed him, the session of 13th Street Presbyterian listened to Simpson and his dreams for evangelism and a missionary magazine, but in fact they were not prepared to absorb his vision and its meaning to their particular church.

The pastor was moving too fast and too far. When he brought 100 Italian converts as applicants for membership to the session, they flatly refused. Such a revolutionary invasion was not acceptable to the social and cultural status of 13th Street Church.

This frustration of his vision combined with his ambitious activity of evangelistic preaching in the ghettos and the editorial work on the missionary magazine in addition to his pastoral duties broke Simpson's health. Twice he was forced to take a leave of absence. Several leading medical doctors warned of imminent death from an acute heart condition. On the occasion of his second physical collapse, he went to Old Orchard, Maine, a popular resort and camp ground. Here Dr. Charles Cullis, an Episcopal physician, promoted divine healing along with his clinical practice in Boston.

When exposed to the message of divine healing, Simpson was skeptical, but testimonies he heard there drove him to his Bible. Finally, kneeling alone at a pine log and after a prolonged struggle, a new dimension of Christ's incarnate, risen, glorified reality and fullness emerged in his faith. He was marvelously healed and returned to his ministry at 13th Street Church with new power.

However, soon another problem surfaced. While teaching an adult Sunday School class on First Corinthians 10, a conviction penetrated his heart that as a believer he should obey the Lord in baptism by immersion. He realized baptism to be a symbol of his death to self and sin and a resurrection in union with Christ. Consequently, he was immersed in an Italian Baptist church where his Italian converts attended.

What this would mean to his pastoral ministry he had not resolved, but submissively he reported his action to the New York Presbytery. His argument that a personal obedience should not affect his pastoral duties was rejected. He was not defrocked but he was dismissed from his charge.

If the crisis experience of 1874 was the watershed of Simpson's whole ministry, this was the test of its crucial significance. His dreams for 13th Street Church were shattered. It appears that Simpson wanted to establish a cosmopolitan and metropolitan church like Spurgeon's in London, a larger version of Broadway Tabernacle in Louisville. Now he had no church at all. And the missionary magazine that held great promise in regard to his obedience to the Great Commission had to be sold to another organization.

While still in Louisville, Simpson had also offered himself as a missionary candidate after a traumatic dream, but was pre- vented from going abroad by his wife and children. Now, even his relationship to his wife and children seemed in jeopardy. His brother advised Margaret, Simpson's wife, to leave him because of his apparent eccentricity. How could the family survive in the heart of New York City without income?

Simpson was cast totally on the fullness and sufficiency of Christ. Like Abraham, he was committed to step by step obedience "not knowing whither he went." He felt no bitterness or remorse and exhorted the 13th Street Church to remain loyal and not to follow him explaining he would launch a ministry to evangelize the needy of New York without intending to start a different church.

As Simpson's evangelistic efforts brought converts, however, he could not find churches to disciple transient immigrants. Unexpectantly it became necessary to plant, what he called, a New Testament-patterned church that would adequately meet the needs of converts and support the missionary vision he felt burdened to share with them.

The New York Gospel Tabernacle was founded in 1881 with 17 members and grew to 1,400 by 1900. Had Simpson given his full energy and time to the church instead of to the large variety of interests and organizations that emerged shortly after its founding, its growth would no doubt have been much greater.

The growing church had difficulty finding facilities in New York and relocated eight times in 10 years. It had a large Sunday school program for all ages. Expository preaching, good music and lay involvement by baptized members under the spiritual supervision of elders characterized its services.

Spin-off results by 1900 included two rescue missions, a

cross-denominational missionary magazine published bi-weekly, a missionary training institute of 200 students, a missionary organization of approximately 300 branches and 300 missionaries, a publishing company and book store, an orphanage, a healing home, a hostel for working girls and a home for rehabilitating prostitutes.

In spite of all these developments, Simpson wrote in *The Story of the Christian and Missionary Alliance* (1900): "Its chief methods of work are through local conventions and its printed publications."[9] He also noted that at least 100,000 people were knowledgeably supporting the Alliance. Surely the record between 1874 and 1900 disclosed a remarkable testimony to the reality and power of Christ demonstrated in Simpson's ministry, which the audience in Knox Church could readily recognize.

His Views Solidified

The year 1885 was critical both in terms of developing inter-denominational convention work and for the solidifying of Simpson's convictions regarding sanctification and divine healing. He had made several trips to England mainly to learn and to observe. In 1885 he attended the Bethshan conference, a holiness and healing convention in London sponsored by W.E. Boardman.

Boardman was 74 years of age and in semi-retirement. However, he was president of several Bethshan healing homes in London founded by Mrs. M. Baxter. Like Simpson, he had been influenced by Dr. Charles Cullis, the physician from Boston in the matter of divine healing. The conference convened by Boardman was to explore the relation of holiness to healing.

At this conference Simpson found more than 70 people whose primary ministry involved divine healing. There were

2,500 in attendance from Australia, France, Germany, Holland, Italy, Spain, America and England. On the whole, there were two approaches to sanctification with which he took serious issue when related to healing. One he called "suppressionism" and the other "perfectionism."[10]

The adherents of "suppressionism" held that Spirit-filling but not sanctification was an experience distinct from regeneration. This view was represented in Moody and Whittle. The carnal nature remained after the Spirit-filling but was suppressed by the believer's walk in the Spirit. This doctrine, first promoted by a Brethren movement in England, influenced Moody and was spread in America by what was known as the Prophetic Conference Movement. George C. Needham and James Inglis, initial leaders, had as one of their aims to counter "the ancient heresy of a sentimental higher life."[11] This conference movement between 1878 and 1900 was a formative influence to American evangelicalism. It was associated with what became known as dispensational-fundamentalism.

The other view Simpson could not accept at the Bethshan conference he called "perfectionism." He wrote: "Some of them profess and teach an unscriptural experience of sanctification as state of self-perfection and inability to sin."[12] In 1885, the same year as the Bethshan Conference, the National Holiness Movement held its first General Holiness Assembly and adopted a creed which stated a belief in the entire extinction of the carnal mind, the communication of perfect love to the soul and the abiding indwelling of the Holy Ghost.

Simpson had spoken on previous occasions at the Bethshan conference, but after the various positions were presented he requested special privilege to give an impromptu message. This has since been entitled "Himself" and it became a hallmark for the C&MA.[13] Although too lengthy to repeat, its message was condensed in a lyric:

Once it was the blessing, Now it is the Lord;
Once it was the feeling, Now it is His Word;
Once His gifts I wanted, Now the Giver own;
Once I sought for healing, Now Himself alone.

All in all forever, Jesus will I sing;
Everything in Jesus, And Jesus everything.

Once it was my working, His it hence shall be;
Once I tried to use Him, Now he uses me;
Once the power I wanted, Now the Mighty One;
Once for self I labored, Now for him alone.

Of the leadership at the Bethshan conference Simpson wrote: "The teaching of the convention was always sufficiency, sinlessness and victory by abiding in Christ, but nothingness and worthlessness in self. And there are others, again, who claim peculiar personal gifts, and even power to communicate blessing and divine influence and healing, that lead men away from the work and the Lord Himself, to look to the instrument, and sometimes lead those who claim to be instruments, into the most perilous dangers and extremes, and even into spiritualism itself."[14] The "others" who failed to recognize the centrality of Christ and focused on a "self-empowering" by the Spirit, clearly caused Simpson to see the distinction of his own convictions.

The Centrality of Christ and Sanctification

Though the C&MA was neither a church nor an independent faith mission, its doctrine of sanctification was promoted by interdenominational Bible and missionary conventions and its branch ministry. Emphasis on the fullness of Christ so united its fellowship as to popularize the C&MA as a deeper life and missionary movement. By 1900, it began to look institutional and in an editorial Simpson wrote:

*The permanency of any work chiefly depends, not so much upon
the genius and energy of its founders as upon the question
whether its essential principles are fitted to meet a need in the
hearts of men and to supply a place in the agencies of Christian
usefulness which nothing else fills. It seems to very many of the
friends and advocates of the Alliance that even if its founders and
earliest friends were removed, its great foundation principles
and objects of the greatest importance which are not specially
emphasized by other agencies remain. Especially it holds up to the
aspiration of every Christian the highest possible standard of
Christian life and reveals the secret by which this may be obtained
through the indwelling life of Christ and the power of the Holy
Spirit.*[15]

To Simpson, the strongest element that gave permanence
and substance to the work of the Alliance was its message of
Christ as Sanctifier. He was convinced it represented "the
highest possible standard of Christian life" and that its relevance met the needs of God's people and the church most
effectively.

FOOTNOTES

[1] A.W. Tozer, *Wingspread: Albert B. Simpson—A Study in Spiritual
Altitude,* (Harrisburg: Christian Publications, Inc., 1943), p.
102.

[2] Stanley N. Gundry, *Love Them In,* (Chicago: Moody Press,
1976), p. 158.

[3] Moody's emphasis on power for holy living by the Holy
Spirit should be contrasted to that represented in the National Holiness Association. This latter addressed professing
Christians on the need of a second experience. By the early
1860s, the National Holiness Association listed 304 holiness
evangelists and stated meetings each week. By 1888 four

publishing houses were engaged in publishing holiness materials. By 1892 there were 41 holiness periodicals in circulation. The association was an attempt to bring discipline to divergent views on holiness. Charges of "come-outism" and "no-churchism" became widespread. The association urged Methodist people to remain loyal to their churches. Harold Vinson Synan in *The Holiness-Pentecostal Movement* (Grand Rapids: Eerdmans, 1971), views Pentecostalism as resulting from this movement. Between 1895-1900, scores of denominations were formed from four million Methodists, the largest Protestant denomination in America at that time.

[3] Gundry, Ibid., p. 158.

[4] *Signs Of Our Times*, edited by M. Baxter, clergyman of the church of England, (J. Snow & Co., 2 Ivy Lane, Padernoster Row, June 16, 1875), p. 360. Quote of R. Pearsall Smith: "I have been associated with him (Boardman) in Christian work for perhaps thirty years, and have seen him in many and trying circumstances, yet I have never seen his soul's sabbath broken. I have never seen self expressed in any action."

[5] The Oxford Convention (1874) was followed by the New Brighton Convention in 1875 which was open to all. Attendance swelled to more than 8,000 and has been characterized as the beginning of the Keswick movement. Boardman left for America before the convention and did not become associated with the Keswick movement, though he soon returned to England.

[6] A.B. Simpson, editorial, *The Alliance Weekly.* Oct. 2, 1915.

[7] Ibid.

[8] In his 1859 edition of *The Higher Christian Life*, Boardman stressed the need for a "second experience," but in his 1871 revision this emphasis almost disappears and Boardman explains that though the experience is distinct, it may well occur immediately upon conversion. Note chapter 2, "The Law of Progress," especially pp. 201-209 in the Henry Hoyt

published edition of 1871.

[9] A.B. Simpson, *The Story of The Christian and Missionary Alliance*, p. 6.

[10] Apparently Simpson was more interested in the doctrine of sanctification than divine healing. He once estimated that healing was only "the nickle in the dollar." The terms "suppressionism" and "perfectionism" were existing epithets used in doctrinal controversy. Donald W. Dayton observes: "The epithets the American Holiness movement hurled at Keswick was 'suppressionists' while the Keswick used 'perfectionism.' *The Theological Roots of Pentecostalism*, (Grand Rapids: Francis Asbury Press, 1987), p. 185.

[11] Earnest R. Sundeen, *The Roots of Fundamentalism*, (Chicago: University of Chicago Press, 1970), p. 177.

[12] Simpson, editorial, *The Christian and Missionary Alliance*, July-August, 1885, p. 238.

[13] Simpson's message at the Bethshan conference later entitled "Himself," has been continuously circulated in tract form as representing the message of the C&MA.

[14] A.B. Simpson, *The Christian and Missionary Alliance*, July-August. 1885, p. 238.

[15] A.B. Simpson, *The Christian and Missionary Alliance*, March 31, 1900, p. 20.

3
The Historical Context

The historical context in which truth is revealed and comes to life has a significance that is too often neglected. Jesus Christ came to earth in the fullness of time (Galatians 4:2). The background and continuity of history that preceded His incarnate life and ministry was crucial to an understanding of His mission. The coming of the Holy Spirit on the day of Pentecost followed the earthly life and finished work of Jesus Christ (John 7:39). The dramatic experiences of Pentecost were explained by the Apostle Peter as the result of Christ's glorification in historical and scriptural fulfillment. The early church was not occupied with experiences, *per se*, though experience was important; rather it is said that "they devoted themselves to the apostles' teaching and to the fellowship" (Acts 2:42); objective teaching preceded the subjective fellowship.

The church is designed for a unified expression of faith based on God's self-revelation through the inscripturated Word and history. Historically the Alliance attributes it essential view of sanctification to its founder, Dr. A.B. Simpson. However, its heritage of conviction and corporate character has a larger context and theological background important to its identity and self-understanding.

The vital significance of the centrality of Christ to the sanctifying and filling work of the Holy Spirit was new to Simpson at the time of his crisis experience in 1874. Though he searched long for what seemed lost to the dynamic of Christian living and church life, he was illuminated as he read *The Higher Christian Life* by W.E. Boardman. This, as he testified at Knox Church, resulted in an experience that revolutionized his life and ministry. But experience is essentially truth mediated by the Holy Spirit through biblical revelation and historical continuity. As someone has aptly said, "The difference between a wise man and a fool is not in the degree of experience but in the measure of truth extracted from experience."[1]

Spiritual experience ungrounded in historical theology is temporary and easily distorted by variant winds of teaching. Historians with no Alliance background have confused roots of Alliance doctrine with Keswick or holiness Methodist teaching,[2] both of which are seriously questioned. The church must probe, investigate and guard its doctrine first from Scripture and then from its historical roots to gain unity of faith and maturity or become a cut-flower movement.

The Value of W.E. Boardman's Contribution

No single individual made a larger contribution to Simpson's view of sanctification than W.E. Boardman. Yet, his life and influence has been neglected in proportion to his significance, both in regard to his influence upon evangelicalism as a whole and upon the Alliance in particular.

Simpson's anniversary sermon to Knox Presbyterian Church (see p. 21) recounts the impact produced upon him by his reading *The Higher Christian Life*. The slogans he used throughout his writings to identify the Alliance doctrine of sanctification originated with Boardman. "Christ Himself," "Jesus Only," "the all-sufficiency of Christ" and "Christ's fullness" or "Christ as Savior, Sanctifier and Healer," initially were used by W.E. Boardman.

As previously noted, it was at the 1885 Bethshan conference on holiness and healing, which Boardman promoted and chaired, that Simpson preached the famed "Himself" message and took serious issue with "suppressionism" and "perfectionism." In no other organization or agency has Boardman's view of sanctification been more fully preserved than in the C&MA. Thus, to understand Boardman is to more fully understand Simpson.

No doubt, there were also significant influences behind Boardman, but his view of sanctification was original in the context of his times. This originality together with his self-effacing personality, and the strange turn the Keswick movement contributed, largely explains the failure of historians to acknowledge his special influence.

A Hunger for Sanctification

An understanding that Christ should be made our righteousness and sanctification through the wisdom of God (1 Corinthians 1:30) came to Boardman providentially.[3] He was reared in a rural area along the Susquehanna River of northern New York State where Finney's revivalism had left its mark. Though a minister visited his community occasionally on a circuit, most religious activities in the area were irregular and informal. Despite this, Boardman was soundly converted at age 20 in a revival meeting. He was in private business at the time, and sold it to enter the ministry.

However, shortly after this a cousin proposed to Boardman a business venture by which he said Boardman could earn enough in a year to educate a dozen ministers. Caught up in business, wealth and pleasure, Boardman neglected spiritual things and at age 27 married an unconverted woman.

Soon, however, through a chance remark, Mrs. Boardman learned of her husband's religious background, and Boardman found himself with a lot of explaining to do.

As Boardman recounted his past to his wife, he came under conviction and was restored in fellowship with the Lord. His wife also came under conviction, but Boardman did not know how to help her. She so earnestly sought salvation that she became ill and was confined to bed. During this time they lost a hotel in a fire without insurance and the bank in which Boardman was a partner failed. Convinced he was being chastised for past disobedience, Boardman earnestly sought help while attending church with his wife. As a certain church service drew to a close, his wife came to a complete end of herself and said in her heart that now she could only leave her salvation in God's hands to be saved or lost. Just then, the light broke and she was gloriously converted.

The relief and happiness of Mrs. Boardman shamed her husband. He began to brood over his loss of the joy of salvation. Fortunately, among their personal possessions, Boardman discovered *Memoirs of James Brainerd Taylor.*[4] It was the diary of a young professor at Yale who was dying of consumption but who had kept an account of his experience with God. It was published five years after his death in 1833. A.S. Wilson in *Definite Experience*, describes Taylor as "one of the brightest and most beautiful examples of holiness which has ever adorned the Presbyterian Church." Wilson also records Taylor's own desciption of his experience: "People may call this blessing by what name they please—'Faith of Assurance,' 'Holiness,' 'Perfect Love,' 'Sanctification.' It makes no difference with me whether they give it a name or no name; it contains a blessed reality, and, thanks to my Heavenly Father, it is my privilege to enjoy it."[5]

Seeking such a definite experience as Taylor described, Boardman decided to fast and pray. He continued to do this for six months, often prostrating himself on the floor for hours asking for "the filling of the Spirit."

One day a Methodist minister came to the Boardman home in Potosi, Illinois. Mrs. Boardman was home alone. The minister pressed a book upon her, which he promised to pick up on a return visit. Just before his scheduled return, Mrs. Boardman hurriedly glanced through it and came upon an account of how an Asa Mahan and a Charles Finney were filled with the Spirit. She associated this account with what Taylor had recorded in his diary, and began to understand that Jesus is a full Savior for believers and that the Holy Spirit has been sent to make Jesus Christ all-sufficient for both holiness and life.

Mrs. Boardman was admonished by the visiting minister to give testimony of her experience at a Methodist class meeting. But as she described her discovery in the meeting, the minister interrupted her to say: "Mrs. Boardman, you will not shrink back from professing the whole truth, and calling things by their right names. You'll have to profess perfection or you'll not keep the blessing." Taken back by his remarks she began to argue that she had no perfection to profess and that she had never felt more imperfect. Whereas previously she had thought herself as somebody, now she saw herself as nothing and nobody outside of God's grace and goodness.

The argument continued uncomfortably, but the interchange began to open her husband's eyes. Soon afterward he too experienced "the full presence of Jesus" as two phrases of Scripture fastened upon his mind: "Lo, I am with you alway, even unto the end of the world"; and, "Thou shalt call His name Jesus, for He shall save his people from their sins."[6]

Providentially, it appears, the Boardmans were made to realize that holiness and power were mediated by Christ through the Holy Spirit and that the focus of faith was Christ

Himself. These basic concepts became an anchor to their spiritual liberation and subsequent ministry. Jesus' own indwelling as a present, living Savior and Sanctifier completely changed their outlook. In her biography Mrs. Boardman emphasizes: "We were brought to understand the truth of those words, 'He (the Holy Spirit), shall not speak of Himself; He shall testify of Me.' Yes, He shall reveal to you what I am, so that you may learn My power to keep you, and sin shall not have dominion over you."

The Results of Knowing Christ as Sanctifier

Immediately, the Boardmans started to minister. Soon they sold the business and Boardman was ordained to the ministry. Sensing a need for further training, he entered Lane Seminary in Cincinnati, Ohio. At Lane, he tried to share his understanding of the deeper life with fellow students, but found that the faculty presented a "mountain of difficulty." Soon, however, some of the student leaders sought him out and were spiritually transformed. One student came to Boardman and confessed that while he too wanted Christ in His fullness, he feared the reaction of the faculty and the possibility of jeopardizing a promising future in the ministry. To this Boardman replied:

> *The Holy Spirit has revealed to your heart the true position of things, and you must choose for yourself whether it shall be a life of ups and downs, without joy, without salvation from the power of sin; or a life of blessed continuous victory, with the consciousness of a real personal Savior always with you, making heaven in your soul by His divine presence.*[7]

The young man made a full surrender and became an enthusiastic witness to the lives of other students.

Upon completion of his seminary work, Boardman and

his wife entered upon a period of service to the Lord that often involved hardships and sacrifices. Several years later, while pastoring a Presbyterian church near Philadelphia, Boardman authored the book *The Higher Christian Life*. The book sold faster than publishers could produce them (three companies in England and two in America). One printer sold 60,000 copies within a brief period.

After a period of time in Philadelphia, the Boardmans moved to Los Angeles. Then, during the Civil War, Boardman served with The United States Christian Commission as a chaplain. By the time the war ended, his exhausting schedule had prostrated Boardman, and to recuperate he and his wife went to the mineral waters at Ems, Germany for eight months. During this time he wrote *A Conquering Gospel*.

While in Europe Boardman visited England. There he was hailed as the author of *The Higher Christian Life* and asked to speak at hastily arranged meetings. The response in England was so unanticipated and affirming to their faith, the Boardmans decided to "evangelize believers" with the truth of Christ as Sanctifier. Back in the U.S. they found a response to their work on the eastern seaboard and the central states of America to be overwhelming both in terms of conversions and of believers being led into the fullness of Christ.[8] This brought Boardman to exhaustion again (at retiral age) and back to Ems, Germany.

The Higher Christian Life Movement that came to England through Smith's invitation to Boardman in Germany, came to a climax with a convention at Oxford, England, in 1874. Boardman continued to minister in England and in Sweden, but chose not to attend the New Brighton convention, held in 1875, and left instead for America. Reportedly, the convention was attended by 8,000 people.

The Distinctives of the Higher Christian Life Movement vs. Keswick

Historians trace the beginning of Keswick to the New Brighton convention when T.D. Harford-Battersby, vicar of St. John's, Keswick, promoted the meetings and later that year arranged a similar meeting in his parish.

However, Pearsall Smith acted as the convener, and he clearly saw the meetings at New Brighton as being associated with Boardman's Higher Christian Life Movement. Smith was a wealthy glass manufacturer from Philadelphia whose wife Hannah became renowned for the popular classic, *The Christian Secret of a Happy Life.* He was a lay leader with no formal training in theology, but had been a friend of Boardman for 30 years.[9]

Smith's high profile at New Brighton came to an abrupt end before the concluding sessions. He was advised by a council of eight people appointed by conference leaders to relinquish his leadership and to absent himself from the convention.[10]

In her biography of her husband, Mrs. Boardman glosses over this event. However, after the New Brighton meetings the Higher Christian Life Movement in England was disassociated with Smith and with Boardman, and had a new name. Thereafter it was the Keswick Movement. Not only did the Higher Christian Life Movement thereafter have a new name, it took a new direction doctrinally. Gradually the English Keswick Movement became associated with "the Brethren," a "back-to-the-Bible" movement within the Anglican church. Its strongest representative in England was John Nelson Darby who formulated what was known as dispensationalism. His views were promulgated in America by James H. Brooks, who published several popular books, and C.I. Scofield, who edited the Scofield Bible along with a popular correspondence course.[11]

Scofield, in *Rightly Dividing the Word,*[12] suggests the church age began at Pentecost, and is a parenthetical interlude in which the kingdom promised by Christ and the prophets was postponed. The kingdom was directed to the Jew, not to a Gentile church. The present age of the church is strictly of grace. The church is present essentially in "mystery form" and characterized by "spirituality." In dispensational thought, the indwelling of Christ's fullness in the believer, so central in Boardman and Simpson, is virtually lost; indeed, dispensational leaders considered this emphasis a "sentimental heresy."[13]

Probably the strongest effect of dispensationalism on American evangelicalism and the promotion of Keswick teaching came with a series of prophetic Bible conferences which began in 1878. From 1883 to 1897, such conferences were held annually at Niagara-on-the-Lake, Ontario. They became internationally renowned under Brethren leadership and carried a distinctly dispensational emphasis.

To the popular mind, dispensationalism and fundamentalism became synonymous. The rising tide of liberalism was humanistic, naturalistic and institutionalistic. Liberalism was making its greatest inroads in denominational churches where human improvement and the social gospel was stressed rather than a transforming and transcendent gospel. Concern over the inroads of liberalism made dispensationalism all the more a mark of identification for evangelicalism in America.[14]

Thus, the dominant emphases of the Higher Christian Life Movement were lost by default and not by overt opposition. As it evolved into the Keswick Movement and as Keswick was increasingly influenced by dispensationalism, "Christ Himself" was no longer emphasized. More and more sanctification was associated with the initial act of salvation. The carnal nature of the believer was by nature from earth and to be "suppressed" by the Spirit in this dispensation of the church and of the Spirit. The shift from a Christological emphasis in sanctification to a Pneumatological one associated with "power

for service" becomes prominent in Keswick and in mainstream American evangelicalism. This gave impetus to mainstream Pentecostalism.[15]

The C&MA and the Dispensational Tide

By 1900, the climate in which the C&MA had formerly
thrived was changed, and Simpson began to sense that the
Alliance now stood somewhat alone in its emphases on Christ
as Sanctifier. To his mind this made the C&MA more sorely
needed as a permanent witness on the evangelical scene than
ever before. As far as Simpson was concerned the Alliance position on sanctification had not changed. In his address to General Council in 1905 he reviewed the origin and development
of the Alliance and then added:[16]

> *But far greater than this has been the blessing of a quickened spir-
> itual life into which the teachings of the Alliance have led so many
> of God's struggling children. The testimony which the Holy
> Ghost has given us on this subject has been so different from the
> old traditional ideas of holiness that it has introduced a new
> phase of Christian life. It is not so much our holiness, our sanc-
> tification, our experience and our personal character that Christ's
> disciples are taught to seek, as the All-Sufficiency of the Lord Jesus
> Christ Himself, as a living, personal and indwelling presence,
> and the baptism of the Holy Ghost, as the power that is promised
> to cause us to walk in His statutes and keep His judgments and
> do them.*
>
> *We are taught to look even beyond our sanctification to our
> Sanctifier, and above our blessing to the Blesser, and so to abide
> in Him that we shall be saved from self-consciousness and deliv-
> ered not only from the power of sin, but from the very touch of self.
> This blessed truth of the Christ life, instead of exalting human
> goodness and sanctity, puts us entirely out of sight, claims no self-
> perfection, honors Jesus only, and gives God all the glory. It has
> brought rest to innumerable souls, and left them free from strug-*

*gling and self-consciousness to go forth as ready workers and give
to others the blessing which God has so richly brought to them.*

It is important to note that Simpson's strong emphasis on
what he came to recognize as a unique perspective on sanctification did not isolate Alliance people from the current evangelical milieu or introvert their motivations. A radical identification with Christ set them free from a defensive provin-
cialism or divisive disputation. Admittedly also, dispensational
influences affected many in the Alliance and skewed their
understanding of sanctification from that which the Alliance
continuously had taught. The Scofield Bible became standard fare in Bible Institutes in the 1920s and 30s.

Because of C&MA's interdenominational character, mat-
ters of doctrine and organization were loosely defined and
membership was represented as an informal agreement to
uphold the Fourfold Gospel: Christ as Savior, Sanctifier, Healer and Coming King. Branches were led by superintendents
and not by pastors, the ordinances and regular church discipline were not considered a part of branch function but
belonged to the church.

Though Simpson preferred to characterize the Alliance
doctrine of sanctification as "the deeper life" and Boardman
characterized his as "the higher Christian life," essentially
their views were identical. Neither Boardman nor Simpson
credited his views to any particular man; they believed Scripture
to be the only final rule of faith and practice. Both sought historical and theological continuity as a necessary ballast to
their message. Boardman argued strongly that his basic concepts concerning sanctification were traceable to Martin
Luther, Merle D'Aubigné (Luther's biographer), Jonathan
Edwards (president of Princeton), Richard Baxter (Puritan
leader and writer), John Wesley, Robert Murray McCheyne and
"a host of others." But the message of sanctification had not

been given the emphasis it deserved. Properly integrated, Boardman believed that both antinomianism and self-perfectionism are avoided and the dynamic of Christ's indwelling is released as the person and work of the Holy Spirit is appropriated.

Simpson's belief was similar but he particularly emphasized the significance of the atonement in relation to what he called the "self-life." He also more significantly expressed the application of the fullness and sufficiency of Christ to missions and the church than did Boardman. But historically speaking, Boardman's message of Christ as Sanctifier based on the significance of the incarnation and the atonement was a radical departure from the strong "perfectionist" holiness movement of his day. To see the scriptural nature of the key concepts in Boardman and Simpson and the way such truth is applied becomes important to an understanding of the Alliance and its heritage.

FOOTNOTES

[1] Bernard Ramm, *The Patten of Authority*, (Grand Rapids: Wm. B. Eerdmans Publishing Co., 1957), p. 45.

[2] For example, George Marston, Ernest Sandeen and Robert Mabes Anderson, whose books are documented in this chapter, all identify the C&MA as part of the Keswick movement. The first edition of *The Schaff-Herzog Encyclopedia* identified the C&MA with the Methodist Holiness tradition. Also, more recently, George Verwer, International Coordinator of Operation Mobilization in an unpublished paper entitled "Extremism," p. 3.

[3] The selected background is from *Life and Labours of the Rev. W. E. Boardman*, by Mrs. W.E. Boardman, (London: Bemrose & Sons, 23, Old Bailey; And Derry, 1886).

[4] John Holt Rice, D.D. and Benjamin Holt Rice, *Memoirs of*

James Brainard Taylor, (New York: The American Tract Society, 1833). The book is available at Yale University library.

[5] A.S. Wilson, *Definite Experience,* (London: Marshall & Morgan & Scott, Ltd., n.d.), p. 82.

[6] Mrs. Boardman, *Life and Labours of the Rev. W.E. Boardman,* p. 55.

[7] Ibid., p. 76.

[8] It appears that the area of Boardman's ministry between 1869-1872, became the fertile field for Alliance Branch development between 1887-1900.

[9] Smith's association with Boardman by his own account is narrated in a periodical *Signs of Our Times,* edited by M. Baxter, June 9, 1875, p. 36.

[10] From *The Banner of Holiness,* published Dec. 23, 1875, a periodical with the news item "The Veil Lifted," reveals that a council of eight was appointed by the conference committee to interrogate Smith on an indiscretion to which he confessed. Smith had counseled a lady privately who later spread rumors of affectionate misconduct. After investigation by the council it was determined that nothing immoral or sexually suggestive was intended. J.C. Pollock in *Keswick Story,* (London: Hoddor and Stoughton, n.d.) reveals that the incident was more pathetic than shocking and that the council did Smith disservice by refusing to disclose the facts and to quell the cruel slanders. A son, Logan Pearsall Smith became a professed agnostic and published *A Religious Rebel: The Letters of Hannah Whitall Smith,* the rebel being Logan himself in an effort to vindicate his parents.

[11] C.I. Scofield, *The Scofield Reference Bible,* New edition, (New York: Oxford University Press, 1917). Charles Trumbull stated: "About ten thousand different students, from practically every country on earth and the islands of the sea, studied the correspondence course while Dr. Scofield was personally in charge of it." C.G. Trumbull, *The Life Story of C.I. Scofield,*

(New York: Oxford University Press, 1920), p. 64.

[12] C.I. Scofield, *Rightly Dividing the Word*, (New York: The Bible Truth Press, n.d.).

[13] Ernest Sandeen, *The Roots of Fundamentalism*, p. 177. Sandeen observes that the chief concern among dispensational leaders James Inglis and George C. Needham was "the ancient heresy of a sentimental higher life."

[14] This is documented by George M. Marsden in *Fundamentalism and American Culture*, (New York/Oxford: Oxford University Press, 1980), pp. 118-123.

[15] Robert Mabes Anderson, in *Vision of the Disinherited*, (New York/Oxford: Oxford University Press, 1979), takes issue with Vinson Synan's major thesis in his book, *The Holiness-Pentecostal Movement in the United States*, that the historical lineage of Pentecostalism is to be found in the Wesleyan tradition. "On the contrary," says Anderson, "that wing of the Pentecostal movement which had earlier connections with Wesleyanism became Pentecostal by accepting Keswick (i.e. Calvinist) teachings on dispensationalism, premillennialism and the Baptism of the Holy Spirit." p. 43.

[16] From an annual report of the C&MA, 1905, archival library of the C&MA, Colorado Springs, Colorado.

4
Christ as Sanctifier

When the Pentecostal movement sprang into being in 1906, it had considerable theological support from Wesleyanism and from the American evangelical mainstream for its pneumatological emphasis. In both, the concept of "the baptism of the Spirit" was popularized with ambivalent theological grounding. Pentecostalism cut through the malaise with a simplistic solution: speaking in tongues was a definitive sign of a genuine experience of Spirit baptism.

The Pneumatological Shift

John Fletcher, who with John and Charles Wesley formed the Methodist troika leadership, used the term "the baptism of the Spirit." In the late 1760s, Fletcher wrote to Charles Wesley:

> I am not in the Christian Dispensation of the Holy Ghost and of power. I want for it, but not earnestly enough; I am not sufficiently straitened till my fiery baptism is accomplished. I fear that Dispensation is upon the decline among us. I see few people deeply mourning for the kingdom of the Holy Ghost.[1]

This soul-search of Fletcher for "the kingdom of the Holy Ghost" also gripped Phoebe Palmer in the 1870s. Mrs. Palmer was a Methodist evangelist who is identified by church historians as the progenitor of The National Camp Meeting Association formed in 1867. This was a Wesleyan holiness movement which later became known as The National Holiness Association. Mrs. Palmer, together with her husband published *The Guide to Holiness*,[2] in which sermons and memoirs of the Wesleys and of John Fletcher were reprinted to promote holiness.

By the 1880s, three experiences became normative within the Wesleyan holiness movement: salvation, eradication or Christian perfection and the baptism of the Holy Ghost. A neopentecostal theologian has observed:

> *In early Pentecostalism there was often stress upon Spirit baptism as a third, distinct experience. The first work of God's grace is justification "by which we receive remission of sins"; the second work is sanctification "by which He makes us holy"; whereas "the baptism of the Holy Ghost is a gift of power upon the sanctified life." (Here one sees connections with the Holiness movement of the late nineteenth century that laid stress on sanctification as a "second blessing" and often called it "baptism in the Holy Spirit.") Later classical Pentecostal teaching, however, has increasingly tended to minimize, or even disregard, a second work of sanctification as prerequisite to Spirit baptism; neo-Pentecostals do not stress it at all.*[3]

About 1910, a group developed within Pentecostalism that did not have a Wesleyan holiness background. William H. Durham, a former Baptist minister of Keswick persuasion, promoted the evidence doctrine of speaking in tongues after attending the famed Azusa meetings in 1906. This began a movement that became known as classical Pentecostalism mostly identified as The Assemblies of God which was organized in 1914. The Wesleyan holiness movement broke relations with Pentecostalism in 1912.

It is not surprising to find that classical Pentecostalism found a fertile soil for its development in Keswick teaching.

Though Keswick-dispensationalism had no intention of minimizing the ultimate significance of Christ's incarnation, the dispensational schema nevertheless did so. It taught that Israel and the Church are eternally distinguished and that the kingdom Christ proclaimed was postponed when the Jews rejected their Messiah.[4]

Consequently, the power and authority Christ asserted in the Great Commission after His resurrection was no longer associated with the dynamic of Christ's kingdom but shifted to the Holy Spirit and the "mystery church" in a parenthetical age of grace. The kingdom parables of Jesus were for Israel and not the church.[5] Jesus did not come to establish His church nor was the kingdom extended through the church.

In contrast, Simpson believed that Pentecost revealed the incarnational triumphs of Christ's power and authority to build His church, delegating to it His Great Commission for the establishment of His kingdom. This emphasis on the centrality of Christ was to Simpson a testimony that filled a particular need in American evangelicalism:

> . . . *its great foundation principles and objects of the greatest importance which are not specially emphasized by other agencies remain. Especially it holds up to the aspiration of every Christian the highest possible standard of Christian life and reveals the secret by which this may be obtained through the indwelling life of Christ and the power of the Holy Spirit.*[6]

Christ as Sanctifier in Alliance Theology

That the Alliance should not be confused with Keswick and as part of the fundamentalist mainstream is more easily discerned once the historical and theological context is examined. Its unique contribution to evangelicalism is easily overlooked. But to affirm the undergirding of "Christ as Sanctifier" largely necessitates a reexamination of doctrine concerning the person and work of Christ. Both Boardman and Simpson stressed the incarnational significance of Christ for our sanctification and union with Him as an affirmation of orthodox doctrine and the focus of evangelical dynamic.

Christ the Sanctifier is the God-man. The orthodox doctrine of the Trinity was defined in a series of church councils prompted by controversies that usually surrounded the person of Christ. In this matter the formulation of the Chalcedon creed (A.D. 451) has prevailed. God is eternally one in three persons in which functional subordination exists eternally without effecting equality in essence. When Christ became man, He voluntarily laid aside His rights, privileges and prerogatives as Deity and lived as a man on earth. In dependence on the Father by the Spirit, He lived a sinless human life and by virtue of His holiness and sacrifice became our Savior.

The fact that Jesus Christ was fully God and fully man is essential to salvation. If Jesus were simply a perfect second Adam, He might have died for another man's sin and guilt. But as fully God, Creator and Sustainer of the universe, He died for the sins of the whole world, so that "to all who received him, to those who believed in his name, he gave the right to become children of God" (John 1:12). The penalty of death for sin was paid once for all and in this sense, God the Father sent His Son and gave Him as a sacrifice for the sins of the whole world (1 John 2:2).

This has been called in theology, "passive obedience," a term used by George P. Pardington in distinguishing what he calls a "twofold element in Christ's substitution." One represents Christ's vicarious obedience for sin at Calvary and the other Christ's earthly and human-life obedience for righteousness, or what is called "active obedience."[7]

This twofold element cannot be separated; the second obedience is necessary to the first. It was Christ's life of obedience that enabled Him to be our Sanctifier as well as our initial and ultimate Savior. It was Christ's voluntary obedience which He rendered in all of the temptations and sufferings represented in mankind that made Him a faithful High Priest who could be touched by the feelings of our infirmities (Hebrews 2:18). Simpson wrote:

> *[The cross] lifts us up from sin to righteousness, from the degradation and defilement of our natural condition to the image of Christ and the righteousness of God. "Unto him that loved us, and washed us from our sins in his own blood" is the tribute which every saint has brought to the cross of Christ. Not only does it save, it also sanctifies in a way which lifts us higher than any holiness that Adam ever knew. It sanctifies us by the process of crucifixion and resurrection. It puts not only our past sins, but our sinful nature on the cross with Jesus Christ and are reckoned dead, and then in Christ Jesus we are resurrected and filled with His nature and spirit, so that we become partakers of His holiness and stand in the same place as Christ Himself in spotless holiness and blamelessness before the throne of God.*[8]

Though justification and sanctification cannot be separated, they can be distinguished just as the two elements of obedience cannot be separated but yet distinguished. We receive not only justification and eternal life in the Son but the sanctifying life of the Son. Sanctification is not a form of "suppressionism" because it is Christ's own divine-human life that triumphs in the believer who lives in union with Christ through the Spirit. Simpson wrote: "Christian holiness is not a slow and painful attainment, but a free gift of God, through Jesus Christ, a glorious and present obtainment, received in faith and retained by abiding ever in Him."[9]

Christ is our Sanctifier as the Representative man. Christ represents believers vicariously as man as well as God. The human nature of Christ was not lost in His ascension and glorification. Christ was raised in the flesh. In Him dwells all the fullness of the Godhead bodily (Colossians 2:9).

The human nature of Christ is not to be etherealized even though He is glorified. John, the Apostle, writes: "That which was from the beginning, which we have heard, which we have seen with our eyes, which we have looked at and our hands have touched—this we proclaim concerning the Word of life. The life appeared; we have seen it and testify to it, and we proclaim to you the eternal life" (1 John 1:1-2). He is forever man as well as God.

When God created man in His own image, He gave man dominion in creation; he was to subdue it and fill it (Genesis 1:26). The Psalmist declared: "The highest heavens belong to the LORD,/ but the earth he has given to man" (115:16). Man is a trustee and steward under God.

However, Satan usurped the authority given to man. He became a squatter on man's rights, privileges and prerogatives. Satan is "the ruler of the kingdom of the air, the spirit who is now at work in those who are disobedient" (Ephesians 2:2).

Jesus, as Son of Man, overcame Satan in temptation and challenged his authority while fulfilling the will and purpose of the Father. Finally, through the cross He conquered all of Satan's rights, privileges and prerogatives usurped from man. But even before Christ went to the cross, He claimed the authority of the Father for the position He would yet receive through full obedience on Calvary and subsequent enthronement.

The gospels amply illustrate the authority of Jesus. Three incidents in three consecutive chapters in Matthew (7-9) illustrate the authority Jesus exercised. In Matthew 7 "the crowds were amazed at his teaching, because he taught as one who had authority, and not as their teachers of the law" (Matthew 7:28-29).

In chapter 8, a centurion pled with Jesus to heal his servant paralyzed and in terrible suffering. Jesus said that he would go and heal him. The centurion protested that he was not worthy that Jesus should come under his roof: "just say the word, and my servant will be healed. For I myself am a man under authority, with soldiers under me. I tell this one, 'Go,' and he goes; and that one, 'Come,' and he comes. I say to my servant, 'Do this,' and he does it" (8:8-9). At this, Jesus was astonished and said that He had not seen such great faith in anyone in Israel. The centurion believed Jesus was under a much higher authority than Caesar, and he put his full weight of faith in Him.

In Matthew 9, a paralytic was brought to Jesus lying on a mat. When Jesus saw the faith of the men who brought him, He said to him, "Take heart, son; your sins are forgiven" (9:2). The teachers of the law thought this was blasphemy, for only God can forgive sins. Then Jesus, knowing their thoughts, said, "Which is easier: to say, 'Your sins are forgiven,' or to say 'Get up and walk'?" Then Jesus said, "But so that you may know that the Son of Man has authority on earth to forgive sins. . . . Get up, take your mat and go home" (9:5-6).

As obedience and submission meant authority and power for Jesus, so it is in our submission to and union with Christ. The parallelism is not only a matter of following an example but an identification with Christ that includes the disposition of the heart. As one theologian has observed: "Unlike other men, He (Christ) did choose to be perfectly obedient to God's will. Moreover, this obedience consisted in more than a mere pattern of conduct; it included a disposition of the heart"[10] The disposition of Jesus toward the Father and union with Him must be ours toward Christ.

Jesus drew three parallels as a challenge to His disciples. First, "As the Father has loved me, so have I loved you. Now remain in my love. If you obey my commands, you will remain in my love, just as I have obeyed my Father's commands and remain in his love" (John 15:9-10). The Apostle Paul could say, "I have been crucified with Christ and I no longer live, but

Christ lives in me" (Galatians 2:20). Paul had signed a death-warrant on all his own rights, privileges and prerogatives. What Christ accomplished for Paul on the cross, was also wrought in him.

But the apostle also goes on to say, "The life I live in the body, I live by faith in the Son of God, who loved me and gave himself for me" (2:20). Love and obedience to Christ's commands were two sides of the same coin for Paul even as it was in Christ's relationship to the Father.

Secondly, Jesus drew a parallel of the glory the Father had given Him which He would now give His believers: "I have given them the glory that you gave me, that they may be one as we are one: I in them and you in me. May they be brought to complete unity to let the world know that you sent me and have loved them as you have loved me" (John 17:22-23). Effective witness to the world comes from the glory Christ gives to those unified with Him. His own magnificence and grandeur produces corporate unity and effective witness.

Thirdly, Jesus drew a parallel of sentness. "Again Jesus said, 'Peace be with you! As the Father has sent me, I am sending you.' And with that he breathed on them and said, 'Receive the Holy Spirit'" (20:22-23). The sentness of believers into all the world follows in pattern the work of Christ who accomplished His work by the Holy Spirit (Matthew 12:28). Without this, missions becomes a human struggle without peace or an authoritative sentness that comes from the Father and the Son. The parallel Jesus used gives weight and content to pneumatology as well as Christology.

Both Boardman and Simpson saw the dymamic of these parallels very clearly. Simpson wrote:

> *All other systems gave us merely the ideas of things or the commandments or laws which require them of us. But Christ brings the power to realize them and is Himself the reality and substance in our hearts and lives. He is the Great Typical Man. But He is*

> *more than a pattern or a type, exhibiting what we ought to be,
> and demanding our imitation. He is also the Living Head
> and Progenitor of the very life which He Himself exhibits, beget-
> ting it in each of us by a living impartation of His very being,
> and reproducing Himself in us by the very power of His own life,
> and then feeding and nourishing this life by the Holy Spirit out
> of His own being.*[11]

Christ as Sanctifier is the Substitutionary-man. Christ's death not
only effected our substitutionary atonement for sin in penal satisfaction, but His life is our sanctification in substitutionary life-
satisfaction. The cross is not only the answer for death but for
life. These two aspects complement one another when distinguished but not separated.

The Christ-life did not negate the Apostle Paul's self-fulfil-
ment but represented his goal in life:

> *But whatever was to my profit I now consider loss for the sake of
> Christ. What is more, I consider everything a loss compared to the
> surpassing greatness of knowing Christ Jesus my Lord, for whose
> sake I have lost all things. I consider them rubbish, that I may
> gain Christ and be found in him, not having a righteousness of
> my own that comes from the law, but that which is through
> faith in Christ—the righteousness that comes from God and is by
> faith. I want to know Christ and the power of his resurrection and
> the fellowship of sharing in his sufferings, becoming like him in
> his death, and so, somehow, to attain to the resurrection from the
> dead. (Philippians 3:7-10)*

This Scripture would seem to imply that Paul is not sure of
his eternal salvation but this is not what Paul meant to convey.
He desired the fullest measure of Christ's resurrection life
to operate within him while he served Christ here. But such a
life is only realized by conformity to the obedience Christ
rendered in death. In Romans Paul admonishes believers to
"offer yourselves to God, as those who have been brought
from death to life; and offer the parts of your body to him as

instruments of righteousness" (6:13). This is to be a voluntary decision with a disposition that is definite and progressive in spiritual maturity of union.

The fullness of life Paul aimed for was to be found in the resurrection life of Christ now available by the Holy Spirit. This is substitutionary life that comes from the substitutionary-man. Simpson, speaking of a parallel to Paul's expression in Galatians 2:20 with that of the offering of Isaac by Abraham in Genesis 22:1-12 wrote:

> *"I have been crucified with Christ," that is the death of sin; "nevertheless I live," that is the new life in the power of His resurrection; "Yet not I, but Christ liveth in me," that is the offering of Isaac, the deliverance from self, and the substitution of Christ Himself for even the new self; a substitution so complete that even the faith by which this life is maintained is no longer our self-sustained confidence but the very "faith of the Son of God who loved me and gave himself for me," that is, instead of me, and as my Substitute.*[12]

Thus, Simpson believed, even the faith of Christ Himself as substitute-man was imparted by the Holy Spirit. To Simpson there was Pentecost and second Pentecosts to lift the believer to a higher plane of union with Christ. And one must continually receive, moment by moment, between intervals of crisis experiences.[13]

His own discovery of Christ as the substitutionary-man had transformed Simpson's life and ministry. He learned that the Christ who justified also could enter a believer's spirit and substitute His strength, His holiness, His joy, His love, His faith and His power for the believer's weakness and needs. Across the threshold of his spirit there passed a Being as real as the Christ who came to John on Patmos of which he gave testimony during his 50th anniversary celebration of his ordination.

Christ as Sanctifier is the Conquering-man. Christ through the incarnation and the cross conquered sin, self, death and Satan. And a glorious culmination will come to believers and all of creation when Jesus Christ comes again bodily. The glory of the incarnation is not only Christ for us, in us and through us by the cross, but glorification is anticipated in the final consummation when the new heaven and new earth will become one. "For God was pleased to have all his fullness dwell in him, and through him to reconcile to himself all things, whether things on earth or things in heaven, by making peace through his blood, shed on the cross" (Colossians 1:19-20).

Christ's life on earth culminated in the cross which marked a triumph that is yet to be completed when Christ returns, but the benefits of that triumph can already be realized because of His resurrection. Christ Himself is all-sufficient for the accomplishment of His purpose in us. Simpson spoke of such triumphant living as Christ manifest in the flesh again. Christ does not improve us to make us something to be wondered at, but just comes in us and lives as He did Himself on earth.[14]

Christ As Sanctifier and Progressive Revelation

The centrality of Christ threads the unity of divine revelation. The *Christ in the Bible* series by Simpson served as a commentary on the whole Bible though not designed as that. It represented mostly a collation of sermons preached at the New York Gospel Tabernacle in the Scottish Covenanter style of proclaiming "the whole counsel of God." The books of the Old Testament as well as the New were treated sequentially and expositorially.

This was a result of a theological conviction that faith needed the revelation given concerning the whole of creation history. In it the centrality of Christ was progressively revealed. The Bible was given that the foundations of faith might be searched. It was to remind man that God's faithfulness had always been consistent with God's redemptive purpose in Christ. Believers were not a people born yesterday or even of the early church. They were part of God's redemptive purpose since creation.

Christ is the foundation and capstone of a building, the "alpha and omega" that comprehends both the apostles of the New Testament and the prophets of the Old Testament (Ephesians 2:20). This needed to be set forth in fullest meaning because Christianity without its full history is like a man without his childhood.

The fact that there is one God and one Mediator between God and man, the man Christ Jesus (1 Timothy 2:5), was not a truth related only to the New Testament, but applied to the whole of Scripture. That Christ was Savior and Sanctifier for His people with a mission for the whole world was not a narrow truth found in isolated texts but represented the "flesh and bones" of all divine revelation. God was calling out a people to save and sanctify them for His purpose and glory. This was the vantage point from which Christ's fullness and sufficiency was to be understood and received.

Christ as Savior and Sanctifier was a philosophy of history, not mere metaphysical history but creation history. God will fulfill Christ's message of the kingdom; man and creation will culminate in a "restitution of all things." The fitness of salvation and sanctification to the reality of creation will be fully vindicated.

It is against this theological conviction that contrast must be drawn to dispensationalism which taught that God used seven revised plans (caused by human failure) to finally bring man to salvation by grace through faith. God had a different plan for the Jew under the law than for the church under grace. The Keswick-dispensationalist held that believers were baptized into the mystery church and were sanctified at conversion.

set apart 2 Thes 2:13

They could be filled with the Holy Spirit to suppress the carnal nature and to receive power for life and service through an increased yieldedness of faith. Sanctification and suppression was gradual with spiritual growth along with many possible fillings.[15]

The classical Pentecostalist was also a dispensationalist but held that while the new birth baptized believers into the body of Christ the work of the Spirit was not completed in the believer unless the evidence of tongues attended the believer's "Pentecost." The important issue was not salvation, but whether "Pentecost" was complete without the evidence of tongues.

To Boardman and Simpson the issue was God's plan to reveal His Son to the full extent of God's redemptive provision. Though progressive revelation in fulfilment of prophecy was involved, God never changed His plan of redemption. Believers in the Old Testament as well as in the New were justified by faith and are made one in Christ. Many in the Old Testament were filled with the Holy Spirit to fulfill God's calling but the Holy Spirit's person and work was revealed at Pentecost because He was sent by the Father to apply to those who believe what Christ had victoriously accomplished through His incarnation. Temporal history will culminate with Christ's personal coming.

Christ As Sanctifier and the Baptism of the Holy Spirit

In Alliance theology, Christ Himself in redemption is the issue of sanctification and the filling of the Spirit. The Holy Spirit has come to conform the believer to Christ and His fullness. Jesus instructed His disciples that the Holy Spirit would bring glory to Him by taking what was of Him and making it known to them (John 16:14-15). This truth largely determined the Boardmans' understanding of sanctification.

Simpson believed that union with Christ and the filling of
the Spirit were two sides of the same coin.[16] The Holy Spirit
brought to the believer the holiness and fullness of Christ
Himself.

Since the Holy Spirit proceeds from the Father and the
Son and His ministry is to reveal and apply what the Son has
provided for us in the atonement, the Holy Spirit is not an
additive to Christ, but has come to glorify Christ in and
through the believer.

Pentecost revealed that Christ had conquered sin and Satan
and was glorified (John 7:38-39; Acts 2:32-36). Christ's fullness
and union with us by the Spirit is now possible because of the
victory He accomplished in life, death, resurrection and glorification. The Holy Spirit is also the Spirit of Jesus after Pentecost (Acts 16:7). John the Baptist's baptism was a "baptism of
repentance for the forgiveness of sins"(Mark 1:4), but not a
baptism "with the Holy Spirit" (Mark 1:8; John 1:33).

It was at Pentecost that Christ's Lordship and Messiahship
were conclusively and objectively established, and believers are
now to be baptized in the name of Jesus (Acts 2:38). But Jesus
as Lord and Christ has also come to baptize and fill with the
Holy Spirit (Acts 1:5-8) all who live in union with Him—not
only representatively but substitutionally and vicariously.

Though this seems explicit from Scripture, the question
regarding the Holy Spirit's witness to Christ as a special enduement of power may not be fully satisfied. Certainly the Holy
Spirit witnesses to Christ as the conquering-man, but the special need of enduement for service and power as promised in
Acts 1:8 seems to call for further explanation. Simpson was
opposed to the belief that one could possess the Holy Spirit as
his own superior power;[17] rather it was Christ through the
Spirit possessing us.

The answer is suggested by John Dahms, a professor in
New Testament, in the following:

Why did effective witness to Christ require a special endowment with power? We suggest that it was because "Christ crucified (is) a stumbling block to Jews and folly to Gentiles" (1 Corinthians 1:23), a much greater stumbling block and folly than anything in the message of the Old Testament, or even in the public teachings of Jesus. Though the Old Testament and the teachings of Jesus emphasize that salvation is by grace (e.g., Deut. 7:6ff; Ps. 32:1ff; 51:1ff; Zech. 4:6; Luke 15:18-32; 18:9-14), the New Testament understanding of the significance of the cross in relation to grace is far more offensive to the natural man than any doctrine previously proclaimed. If there is to be effective witness to Christ, it is necessary that the Spirit witness particularly to Him (in support of the witness of those who were His) as John 15:26 promises. It is significant in this connection that the Spirit convicts the world of sin, because they do not believe in Christ, of righteousness because Christ has gone to the Father and we see Him no more; of judgment, because the prince of this world was judged at Calvary (John 16:8-11; cf. 12:31). We suggest that it was only as the Spirit of Christ that the Spirit could bring such conviction concerning Christ and the significance of His death, resurrection and ascension.[18]

This explanation helps to clarify the need for recognizing and by faith trusting the person and work of the Holy Spirit for effective ministry as well as for sanctification. While Boardman does not seem to touch on this and Simpson does not make this kind of distinction, he certainly did believe in trusting the Holy Spirit's anointing for service. Simpson observed that according to Ephesians 3:20, Colossians 1:29 and Philippians 3:21, God did work in two directions, first in the believer's heart and secondly in the sphere of providence and government. But, "the one must ever keep pace with the other." Anointing for service can only be as effective as it is matched, " according to the power that works in us" as expressed in Colossians 1:29.[19]

Christ As Sanctifier and the Crisis of the Deeper Life ~ *P.*₂₄

The founder of the Alliance and his leaders contended strongly for a Spirit-filled life marked by a crisis of faith. It was not that the crisis or the filling was a matter of feeling or chronology. However, in full salvation sanctification was distinguished from other aspects of Christian experience. Pardington believed that the reception of the Holy Spirit's fullness could occur at conversion or subsequent to conversion. The issue was that Christ in His fullness must be perceived and the Spirit's ministry for this must be received by the believer. He wrote:

> *Indeed, where there is right Scriptural teaching no interval of time need occur after conversion before the Holy Ghost is received. Unfortunately, however, this is seldom the case. Generally an interval of time—and often it is a long period—does occur . . . We cannot refrain from saying that we believe God never intended that there should be a barren waste of Christian experience between regeneration and sanctification, but that conversion should be immediately followed by a life of victory over sin and self in union with the indwelling Christ and through receiving the gift of the Holy Ghost.*[20]

Simpson wrote similarly:

> *We are willing, however, to concede that the baptism of the Holy Ghost may be received at the very same time a soul is converted. We have known a sinner to be converted, sanctified and saved all within a single hour, and yet each experience was different in its nature and was received in proper order and by a definite faith for that particular blessing. What we contend for is that the baptism of the Holy Spirit is a distinct experience, and must be received by a definite faith, and this involves the crisis: a full surrender and an explicit preparation of the promise of God by faith.*[21]

The experience of Christ as Sanctifier required the filling of the Spirit or the baptism of the Spirit or the reception of the Spirit. To claim the latter without recognizing the need of the former was a form of godliness without power. The Holy Spirit's power was the power of Christ's resurrection and ascension.

How well Christ in His fullness is perceived will vary from one believer to another, but in the order of salvation He must be perceived as Sanctifier as well as the Baptizer of the Holy Spirit. Simpson believed that the effects of divine filling was the secret of holiness:

> *There is a measure of the Holy Spirit's life in every regenerate soul, but it is when every part of our being is filled with His love and possessed for His glory that we are wholly sanctified, and it is this divine fullness which excludes and keeps out the power of sin and self, even as it was the descending cloud upon the tabernacle which left no room for Moses within.*[22]

The Scriptures use the picture of marriage to describe our relationship to God. To some, earthly marriage is a contract to abject slavery, while to others it is the bliss of heaven. To describe the transition from the former to the latter is elusive. Yet similarly, when one has learned and experienced the gracious goodness and satisfying fullness in Christ, the relinquishment of one's own rights, privileges and prerogatives becomes a privilege and not a duty. The provision and appropriation of the Holy Spirit's person and work becomes not only a comfort but a joyful aspiration. In Alliance theology this was to know "Christ as Sanctifier."

Simpson, however, visualized not merely the deeper life experience of individual believers, but the corporate oneness in Christ which Jesus spoke of when he prayed: "My prayer is not for them alone. I pray also for those who will believe in me through their message, that all of them may be one, Father, just

as you are in me and I am in you. May they also be in us so that
the world may believe that you have sent me" (John 17:20-21).

FOOTNOTES

1 Vinson Synan, *The Holiness-Pentecostal Movement*, p. 77.
2 Dr. and Mrs. Palmer published *The Guide to Holiness* in 1865
   and by 1870 reached a circulation of 40,000. George Marsden
   in *Fundamentalism and American Culture*, p. 74, claims that Mrs.
   Palmer's work as evangelist and publisher led to the foundation in 1867 of the influential Camp Meeting Association for the Promotion of Holiness, out of which the sepa-
   ratistic holiness movement grew.
3 J. Rodman Williams, *The Pentecostal Reality*, (Plainsfield, NJ:
   Logos International, 1972), p. 62. Williams was professor of
   Systematic Theology at Austin Presbyterian Theological
   Seminary, Austin, Texas.
4 C.I. Scofield, *Rightly Dividing the Word of Truth*, p. 13.
5 C.I. Scofield (ed.), *The Scofield Reference Bible*, p. 1227.
6 A.B. Simpson, *The Christian and Missionary Alliance*, March 31,
   1900, p. 204.
7 George P. Pardington, *Outline Studies in Christian Doctrine*,
   (Harrisburg: Christian Publications, Inc., n.d.), p. 277.
8 A.B. Simpson, *The Cross of Christ*, (Harrisburg: Christian
   Publications, Inc., 1910), p. 54.
9 A.B. Simpson, "Distinctive Teachings," *The Alliance Weekly*, May
   16, 1925, p. 335.
10 David Buschart, "The Obedience of Christ: A Study in Biblical and Systematic Theology," unpublished paper, May,
   1983, p. 40.
11 A.B. Simpson, *A Larger Christian Life*, (Harrisburg: Christian Publications Inc., n.d.), p. 42.
12 Ibid., pp. 69-70.
13 Ibid., p. 46.

[14] A.B. Simpson, *The Fourfold Gospel*, (Harrisburg: Christian Publications, Inc., 1925), p. 38-39.

[15] For a fuller description of the development in Keswick-dispensational thought regarding the baptism of the Spirit, see Robert Mabes Anderson, *Vision of the Disinherited*, p. 43ff.

[16] A.B. Simpson, *The Alliance Weekly*, Dec. 20, 1919, p. 212.

[17] A.B. Simpson, editorial, *The Christian and Missionary Alliance*, July-August, 1885, p. 238.

[18] John Dahms, "The Significance of Pentecost," unpublished paper, Dec. 31, 1989, p. 12.

[19] A.B. Simpson, *A Larger Christian Life*, pp. 133-134.

[20] George P. Pardington, *Outline Studies*, p. 163.

[21] A.B. Simpson, *Living Truths*, Dec. 1905.

[22] A.B. Simpson, *A Larger Christian Life*, p. 46.

5
Sanctification and the Cross

Facing complex problems of immorality, carnal living and misguided enthusiasm over the gifts of the Spirit, the Apostle Paul began his letter to the Corinthian Christians by laying down some ground rules. He instructed the Corinthian congregation to examine their attitudes of self-wisdom, self-strength and pride. He reminded them that it was of God that they were in Christ Jesus, "who has become for us wisdom from God—that is, our righteousness, holiness and redemption." He testified to a singular purpose: "For I resolved to know nothing while I was with you except Jesus Christ and him crucified" (1 Corinthians 1:30-2:2).

In 1906, when Pentecostalism swept Indiana and Ohio in particular, the threat of misguided enthusiasm regarding spiritual gifts and the need to reexamine Alliance doctrine took on new dimensions. Having been content to exist as an interdenominational missionary society and as a loose-knit organization of informal members in the branches the Alliance was particularly vulnerable to Pentecostal defection.[1] A pre-Council conference was arranged in May, 1906, which gave special consideration to a position paper prepared by George Pardington. This later appeared in book form as *The Crisis of the Deeper life.*

In his paper Pardington reminded the conference of Alliance workers that the Alliance had neither a formal creed nor an official confession of faith because it was in substantial accord with evangelical truth "and in common with the various denominations accepts the great body of Protestant theology." But to identify the special calling and distinctive testimony of the Alliance, he referred to a promotional statement in general use at the time:

> *Pre-eminently we are witnesses to Christ. We are glad to testify to Him before we speak of any of His blessings or gifts to men. It is Christ as a Person, as a living reality, as the supreme fact of history and life, Jesus Himself, Who is the theme of our testimony. Soon He is to appear in the vivid and glorious revelation of His personal majesty, filling all earth and heaven. . . . Above everything else this is a Christ movement. If we are saved it is Christ who saves us. If we are sanctified it is Christ who is made unto us sanctification. . . . To give salvation to the sinner; to make Christ real to the believer; to present Christ in His fullness through the power of the indwelling Holy Ghost as the complete satisfaction of every need of spirit, mind, and body; to give Christ and the riches of His grace to the heathen world;—this is our special calling and distinctive testimony.*[2]

The Two Aspects of the Cross

Implicitly, Pardington's emphasis on the "crisis of the deeper life" was in answer to the Pentecostal emphasis on "the baptism of the Holy Ghost." Specifically he related this crisis to the cross and a particular view of the atonement. In his *Outline Studies in Christian Doctrine* he explains the Alliance view specifically in contrast to five other views and calls it the "Substitutional, or Satisfaction Theory of the Atonement"; this theory, the first suggestions of which are found in the writings of Augustine (4th century), was elaborated by John Calvin (16th century), and is today held by the Reformed and Presbyterian theologies. It is commonly known as Calvinism; sometimes it is called the "Orthodox Theory," or "Ethical Theory." It is, we believe, the true scriptural view.[3]

This view is basic to Alliance doctrine of Christ as Sanctifier. The transforming power of Christ is made operative by the cross. His life is made relevant—spiritually, ethically and dynamically—by the cross.

The Holy Spirit can produce nothing for us, in us or through us except on the basis of who Jesus is and what the cross made possible. The atonement includes everything Christ is to us and the highest work of the Spirit is to make Christ experimentally real and effective to the believer's need. But it is Christ Himself who is the real food and drink: "The work of God is this:" said Jesus, "to believe in the one he has sent. . . . This bread is my flesh, which I will give for the life of the world. . . . For my flesh is real food and my blood is real drink" (John 6:29, 51b, 55).

Christ's atonement represented two aspects, as Pardington explains:

> *The theory holds to a twofold element in Christ's substitution, namely: a vicarious obedience (known theologically as "active obedience") for righteousness, and a vicarious punishment (known theologically as "passive obedience") for sin. Thus Christ takes the place of sinners in both penalty and precept, and, as their substitute, endures the punishment which on account of sin they deserve, and in His obedience fulfils the righteousness required of them."*[4]

Pardington recognized two corresponding aspects of holiness, the one he called the *historical* and the other *experimental.* The historical resulted from the finished work of Christ in redemption explained in *Outline Studies* as "passive" obedience. This was judicial and positional, representing the death side of the cross. The experimental he explained as that wrought in the believer's heart and life by the Holy Spirit as a result of Christ's active obedience—the obedience Jesus rendered to the Father in His life upon earth. This obedience gave efficacy to the cross for our salvation and His enthronement made resurrection life possible to the believer by the Holy Spirit. The Holy Spirit does not provide an additive to the life of Christ but makes Christ's very life as lived in human form real to us.

The relationship of the death side to the life side of the cross meant that sanctification was not separated from justification. The "crisis" was the need for the believer to die to self as well as sin, and by His grace to so actualize an identification with Christ's death in vicarious consecration that Christ's resurrection life might pervade the believer by the Holy Spirit.[5]

The need to emphasize the cross in these two aspects for sanctification became especially needful in the unruly climate of the day. Pardington observed: "The attempt to divorce judicial holiness from experimental holiness is always attended by consequences more or less disastrous to moral character and conduct. Of sanctification as well as of marriage is it true—'What God has joined together, let no man put asunder.'"[6]

In the teaching of Boardman and Simpson as in Pardington, the believer must identify himself fully with Christ by actively reckoning himself dead indeed to sin and self and alive to Christ through the cross, appropriating the person and work of the Holy Spirit as applying the resurrection life of Christ. They believed that those who looked upon sanctification as being synonymous with regeneration inevitably sought initial salvation by grace through faith but resorted to good works for sanctification. For that reason many believers become weak and defeated trying to live the Christian life by their own strength.[7]

Boardman, chiding the Oberlinians (followers of Finney) and the Wesleyans (Wesleyan Holiness) about their claim of perfectionism, says, "Now what is the right and the truth of the matter? Exactly what is attained in this experience? Christ. Christ in all his fullness. Christ as all in all. Christ objectively and subjectively received and trusted in. That is all. And that is enough."[8]

Simpson in a series on the Gospel of John makes a similar comment: "It is just as wrong to stop at the cross (for penal satisfaction) as it is to stop before the cross. . . . Christ's death is only the background for His resurrection. . . . It is the life of Jesus Christ, His risen life as well as His atoning death, which cleanses us from all sin. We are 'saved by His life,' quite as truly as by His death."[9]

There is a death side and a life side to the cross. Christ's passive obedience in penal satisfaction is not sufficient by itself and though in regeneration the believer receives the life side, he must come to recognize Christ as his Sanctifier in his appropriation of the Holy Spirit to bring the objective and subjective into proper balance.

The Objective and Subjective Aspects of the Cross

Between 1905 and 1910 the Alliance was influenced strongly by the teaching of F.E. Marsh of Sunderland, England, who became associate pastor to Simpson at the New York Gospel Tabernacle. He also lectured at The Missionary Training Institute and was lauded by Simpson as "one of the most orthodox, spiritual and able writers and preachers of the best school of Christian teachers in England."[10] His lectures on the atonement were collected in a book entitled *The Greatest Theme in the World.*

Marsh observed that "some are preaching the subjective side of the cross alone, and omitting the objective."[11] Faith is based on facts revealed in and through an objective creation since "The wrath of God is being revealed from heaven against all the godlessness and wickedness of men who suppress the truth by their wickedness. . . . For since the creation of the world God's invisible qualities—his eternal power and divine nature—have been clearly seen, being understood from what has been made, so that men are without excuse" as Romans 1:18 and 20 reveal. Faith rests on God's inspired Word that has been objectively given by inspiration. But most clearly and dynamically, faith is based on Christ manifested in the flesh, a life given on a cross at Calvary in real history. "Christ crucified," says Marsh, "is the greatest theme in the universe, for it proclaims the greatest work ever performed by the greatest Person, and secures the greatest possible ends."[12]

Without the objective aspect of the cross, the subjective becomes hollow and loses its significance. The objective must precede the subjective. Christ saves us by who He is before He can save us by what He does. Marsh writes: "We must have the rock smitten before the stream flows, the sun before the sunshine, the tree before the fruit, the root before the plant, the foundation before the building, the cause before the effect and the producer before the product."[13]

On the other hand, Marsh says, "Some are preaching the objective side of the cross of Christ's atonement and omitting the subjective power of it." This was the fault of much evangelism that Marsh observed. The Word was proclaimed but results were not seen or expected. Holiness was preached, but transformation was not effectively demonstrated. In his typical mode of expression he writes: "The root is the cause of the tree, but a tree which is all root is only a stump; . . . the foundation is the base of the house, but the house which is all base is an unfinished product; and the vine which is fruitless is only fit for the fire."[14]

The need for balance is so stressed by Marsh that he finally sets forth 26 parallels of the objective and subjective. This apparently came from his desire to see the truth of sanctification as spiritually balanced in Christ's ongoing redemptive work and not merely as a power-zap experience in the baptism of the Spirit.

This view of the atonement corresponded essentially with the understanding of Boardman and Simpson, but it came into fresh significance as subjective experience was stressed at the expense of objective truth when the wave of Pentecostalism swept the evangelical world like an avalanche from 1906 to 1908. The background to the Alliance approach regarding the atonement is probably the classical work produced by George Smeaton, professor of Systematic and Exegetical Theology at Edinburgh, Scotland, the parent school of Knox College from which Simpson graduated. He wrote *The Doctrine of the Atonement as Taught by Christ Himself* (1868) and *The Doctrine of the Atonement as Taught by the Apostles* (1870). One of the best treatments of Christ's incarnation is by James Orr, *The Christian View of God and the World*, published in 1893. He is identified as "the leading United Presbyterian theologian at the time of the United Free Church of Scotland union of 1900, and beyond his

own church and nation he came to exercise significant influence in North America."[15] Orr asserted that a complete view of
Christ's work:

> . . . *will include the fact that in the Incarnation a new Divine life
> has entered humanity; . . . will include the fact of a holy and per-
> fect and continuous surrender of Christ's will to God, as an offer-
> ing, through the Eternal Spirit, in humanity, of that which
> man ought to render, but is unable in his own strength to
> give—the presentation to God in humanity, therefore, of a perfect
> righteousness, on the ground of which humanity stands in a new
> relation to God, and is accepted in the Beloved.*[16]

The incarnate, active obedience of Christ as man's provi-
sional ground for sanctification through the atonement col-
ored the Scottish-Puritan tradition. In contrast, the dispensational school which so strongly affected American evangelicalism early in the 20th century, denied the significance of
Christ's active obedience to the atonement. As observed by
David Buschart, theology professor at Canadian Theological
Seminary, Louis S. Chafer, representing classical dispensationalism in his *Systematic Theology*, ". . . is among those who
deny any immediate soteriological significance to Christ's life-
time of obedience."[17] Thus dispensationalism separated Christ
from the Holy Spirit. This undermined the Christ Himself
message of the C&MA. This apparently prepared the way for
the subjectivistic excess around 1906.[18]

The Holistic Context of the Atonement

Sanctification is best understood in terms of the full scope
of Christ's redemptive work. Pardington stressed that redemption by the cross represents a balance between the historical
and the experimental. Marsh emphasized the need for the
objective and the subjective. Simpson said there is a death and

life side to the cross. However, the question remains as to the true significance of sanctification in God's total plan of redemption.

In Keswick-dispensationalism and later in classical Pentecostalism and in neo-Pentecostalism, there was a marked decline of emphasis on the doctrine of sanctification. As J. Rodman Williams, a neo-pentecostal theologian of the Presbyterian church has observed:

> *Later classical Pentecostal teaching . . . has increasingly tended to minimize, or even disregard, a second work of sanctification as prerequisite to Spirit baptism; neo-Pentecostals do not stress it at all. . . . Sanctification (in its initiatory stage) is understood as being included in conversion, or is thought of as a lifelong process that may or may not include Spirit baptism.*[19]

The apparent assumption in the movements mentioned above is that the baptism of the Spirit by its very nature is the work of the *Holy* Spirit and therefore sanctification as a work of Christ is minimized and credited to the Spirit. But the Holy Spirit proceeds from the Father and the Son, and only in that order to take the things of Christ and to reveal and to apply them. Thus the full scope of Christ's work is significant and must be seen in progressive relationships. Marsh states that "The death of Christ is the causative power which produces a corresponding action."[20]

The arranged description below is an attempt to illustrate the nature and scope of Christ's redemptive work on the cross. Corresponding relationships are arranged as implicit to the substitutionary view of the atonement expressed by Simpson, Pardington or Marsh. This integration helps to clarify what appears appropriate although no claim of direct source is made. This comprehensive scope as projected is not exhaustive nor does it include all of Marsh's corresponding parallelisms. Rather, the progression serves to illustrate Christian experience in relation to the cross:

The Death Side of the Cross THE HISTORICAL, OBJEC- TIVE AND FINISHED WORK OF CHRIST IN THE ATONE- MENT.	The Life Side of the Cross THE EXPERIMENTAL, SUB- JECTIVE AND LIFE WORK OF CHRIST IN THE ATONE- MENT.
Objective Reconciliation by Propitiation: The wrath of God is appeased by expiatory sacrifice (1 John 2:2), ". . . so we may die to sins and live for righteousness" (1 Peter 2:24).	*Subjective Reconciliation by Grace through Faith:* God is reconciled. The rent veil provided a new and living way through His body (Hebrews 10:19-20).
God's Objective Calling: Through nature and man's conscience, the Word and the historical work of Christ, all are called to salvation (Romans 1:18-20; 2:15; 10:8-9, 14-17).	*God's Subjective Calling:* The Spirit convicts of sin, righteousness and judgment to bring repentance and faith for salvation (John 16:8-10; 1 Corinthians 1:23-24).
Justification: Christ historically fulfilled the moral and ceremonial law as representative man with the power to declare believers righteous and positionally sanctified (Romans 5:12; 8:30).	*Regeneration:* Christ's own righteous life given on Calvary is made available by the Holy Spirit (Titus 3:3-7; Acts 2:37-41; 5:30-32).
Adoption: Through justification we have the legal right to be children of God and adopted into God's family (John 1:12; Galatians 4:5).	*Sonship:* Through regeneration and the witness of the Spirit we have assurance as Sons (Galatians 4:6; Romans 8:15-16).
Identification with Christ: By active reckoning ourselves dead to sin and self we find our freedom and life in total submission (Romans 6:11, 13-14; 8:1-2; 12:1-2).	*Union with Christ:* Enjoying His fullness and riches by appropriating the Holy Spirit's person and work (John 15:4-5; Ephesians 5:18).

Though the scope of Christ's redemption through the cross is not exhaustively described in this diagram, it serves to illustrate how Christ crucified, risen again and ascended to the Father is made relevant to the need of man by the Holy Spirit as perceived in Alliance theology.

A deeper work of the Holy Spirit brings believers into identification and union with Christ. His life and fullness becomes ours by the Holy Spirit. Oswald Chambers expresses the truth succinctly: "It is not the baptism of the Holy Ghost which changes men, but the power of the ascended Christ coming into men's lives by the Holy Ghost that changes them. We too often divorce what the New Testament never divorces. The baptism of the Holy Ghost is not an experience apart from Jesus Christ; it is the evidence of the ascended Christ."[21]

A.B. Simpson related the baptism of the Spirit and union with Christ in these words:

> *The divine agent in this blessed experience is the Holy Spirit. It is His province to reveal the Lord Jesus to us as our Sanctifier, and then to minister Him to us moment by moment for the supply of every need in our spiritual life. Therefore, the baptism of the Holy Spirit is simultaneous with our union with the Lord Jesus; the Spirit does not act apart from Christ, but it is His to take of the things of Christ and show them unto us.*[22]

Emphasis on the cross became strong in Simpson's ministry between 1907 and 1910. Simpson preached a series on the cross which were put into a book entitled, *The Cross of Christ,* published in 1910. He sensed the absence of this emphasis in what many evangelicals were teaching. Pentecostalism seemed to be espousing either a form of modalism in which Christ was absorbed into the Holy Spirit or a form of Tritheism in which Christ and the Holy Spirit were not only distinguished but separated. It was not uncommon to hear Pentecostals contrast salvation as a Paschal gift and the baptism of the Spirit as a Pentecostal gift, as though these were not only separate but also graduated. This is contrary to both the Chalcedonian and the Athanasian Creeds of the early church. But as the significance of the cross was stressed in the Alliance, the work of Christ and the power of the Spirit were related and made relevant.

Sanctification and the Message of the Cross

But the question may still be asked, why be so Christ-centered when surely the three persons of the Godhead are equal? Since the Holy Spirit proceeds from the Father and the Son, can we not be Pneumatics as well as Christians? We begin our faith in Christ, do we not also begin "in the Spirit"? We are saved by Christ but are we not also regenerated by the Spirit? We are sanctified by Christ, but are we not also sanctified by the Spirit? So why stress Christ as Sanctifier?

If we comprehend the message of the cross, these questions will be answered. Christ's agony in Gethsemane was not due to His anticipated death; it was the reason He came in the first place. The agony was caused by His bearing the needs of man in His body. He identified fully with our weakness and finally with our sin. Had he come through this agony as Son of God only, He would have been unable to call us brothers, unable to succor us in temptation, unable to save us and sanctify us. But He came to assume our nature and to make us partakers of His divine nature.

Christ has entered fully into our humanity that we might enter into His and find a human-divine life suited to our need. This is what caused Boardman to exclaim with fervor: "It suits me exactly, and I would not be without it for worlds; it is just as if you put a bird into the air or a fish into the sea. God has put me into the element for which I was created."[23]

The message of the cross is that earthly living represents the highest opportunity in preparation for heaven. To live in a fallen world by the Spirit of Christ conforms us to His image, the image He fulfilled on the cross—"to become like Him in His death"—that is the highest challenge! Our participation in His resurrection life is always contingent on our participation in His death. This is not the language of escapism but the language of involvement. The goal of every Spirit-filled Christian is to become like Jesus through His imparted nature.

It seems doctrinaire for Simpson to speak of "Jesus Only." This obviously is an expression open to misunderstanding. But in the total context of his theology regarding Christ and the cross it had a deep and special meaning:

Jesus only is our message,
Jesus all our theme shall be;
We will lift up Jesus ever,
Jesus only will we see.

Jesus only is our Saviour,
All our guilt He bore away,
All our righteousness He gives us,
All our strength from day to day.

Jesus is our Sanctifier,
Cleansing us from self and sin,
And with all His Spirit's fullness,
Filling all our hearts within.

Jesus only is our power,
He the gift of Pentecost;
Jesus, breathe Thy power upon us,
Fill us with the Holy Ghost.[24]

Only man, in all of creation, is modeled after God's likeness. Only the Son of God became man to make man God-like. God's purpose in redemption is not to redesign us as though He made an initial mistake in the way He formed us. He was completely pleased with man's original state. But it was a perfection yet to be completed. During Jesus' transfiguration the voice from heaven identified God's design in man nearly completed: "You are my Son, whom I love; with you I am well pleased" (Luke 3:22). In the passion of Christ the completion was still going on, and we hear Him pray in His high-priestly prayer: "For them I sanctify myself, that they too may be sanctified" (John 17:19).

God's solution to man's fall and marred image was not to make him a "superman" through redemption, but to restore man after the image of Christ in full humanness. Therefore, an incipient elitism that cultivates a "holier-than-thou" image is unChristlike, and a spirituality that seeks to escape human reality by divine power is unbiblical.

The cross is a reminder that human life is genuine and eternal. In the cross earth and heaven are bridged for the highest state of development which God designed for human life. To live for one's own ego is to create one's own prison, but to live for Christ and His kingdom opens earth to heaven with all its resources. To deny one's self and to take up the cross and follow Christ is the call of the gospel as we repent of our sins and accept Christ as Savior. But to come to terms with the self-life means crucifixion of one's privileges and prerogatives even as it was for Jesus who sanctified Himself to the Father without reserve. Man's own ideal for himself is not only inadequate but sinful, while God's eternal design is perfect through redemption.

As crucial as commitment was to our Lord in Gethsemane, so crucial will our commitment be in terms of the cross. Pardington seeks to describe the experience:

> *The believer must lay his whole life on the altar, relinquish all right to its control, and count himself henceforth and forever the Lord's. Surrender is a painful act. It means separation; it means sacrifice; it means self-denial; it means death. Before we*

come to Christ as our Savior we learn something of the meaning of surrender. It costs the sinner a good deal to give up the world with its pleasures and attractions. It is hard for him to separate himself from old associates and detach himself from old associations. But when we come to know Christ as our Sanctifier we learn the deeper meaning of surrender. It is one thing to give up the world; it is quite another thing to give up oneself. Yet this is what the Master requires of His disciples: "If any man will come after Me, let him deny himself, and take up his cross, and follow Me." [25]

But the cross has a lifeside as well as a deathside. Christ Himself becomes our Sanctifier and baptizes us with the Holy Spirit to fill us with Himself and to make us instruments for His glory. Man's highest freedom and fulfillment comes about through an obedience that is of divine enabling. God expects believers to accept their humanness as Christ did—in unreserved and voluntary submission through the living Spirit of God. This is the highest challenge for heaven's glory—Christ's own life reissued in human beings here and now. The Holy Spirit is the One who applies the atonement to our need and can produce in us the very nature of Jesus.

FOOTNOTES

[1] Membership cards were used in the Branches. On a 3" X 5" card was recorded a confession of the verbal inspiration of Scripture, the Trinity, Christ's atoning sacrifice through His life, death and resurrection, and the necessity of a regenerating and sanctifying work of the Holy Spirit. The signatory was then asked to subscribe to Alliance teaching of Christ as Savior, Sanctifier, Healer and Coming King, and to support by prayer and giving the worldwide work of the C&MA. It was simply assumed that the applicant understood the distinctive emphases of the C&MA.

² George P. Pardington, *The Crisis of the Deeper Life*, (Harrisburg: Christian Publications, Inc., n.d.), pp. 18-19.

³ George P. Pardington, *Outline Studies in Christian Doctrine*, pp. 277-278.

⁴ Ibid.

⁵ Ibid., pp. 110-112.

⁶ Ibid., p. 112.

⁷ Note Boardman, *The Higher Christian Life*, pp. 45, 52.

⁸ Ibid., p. 58.

⁹ A.B. Simpson, *Echoes of the New Creation*, (Harrisburg: Christian Publications, Inc., n.d.), pp. 48-49.

¹⁰ A.B. Simpson, *The Christian and Missionary Alliance*, March 31, 1900.

¹¹ F.E. Marsh, *The Greatest Theme in the World*, (Glasgow, Scotland: Mesrrs. Pickering and Inglis, 1908), p. 170.

¹² Ibid., Introduction, i.

¹³ Ibid., pp. 170-171.

¹⁴ Ibid., p. 172.

¹⁵ Glenn Scorgie, *A Call for Continuity—The Theological Contribution of James Orr*, (Macon, Georgia: Mercer University Press, 1988), Introduction, p. 1.

¹⁶ James Orr, *The Christian View of God in the World*, (Edinburgh: Andrew Elliot, 1893), p. 317.

¹⁷ David Buschart, "The Obedience of Christ: A Study in Biblical Theology" (unpublished paper), p. 2.

¹⁸ See footnotes in chapter 3 regarding Robert Mabes Anderson. It is enlightening to trace the doctrine of justification in relation to the atonement among early reformers. Luther (1483-1546) saw it as judicial and forensic, objectively accomplished for the believer through faith. Zwingli (1483-1531) based justification on regeneration as a subjective work. Martin Bucer (1491-1551) spoke of two justifications, a primary justification and a moral justification linked by the Holy Spirit. John Calvin (1509-1564) spoke of justification

and sanctification as together representing a union with Christ for moral living. These were not to be separated but needed to be maintained by a life of repentance. This Christological approach was weakened by the Synod of Dort reformulation (1619) in its approach to election and limited atonement.

[19] J. Rodman Williams, *The Pentecostal Reality*, p. 62.

[20] Marsh, *The Greatest Theme in the World*, p. 173.

[21] Oswald Chambers, *My Utmost For His Highest*, (London: Simpkin Marxhall Ltd. 1939 edition). Daily reading for May 27, p. 148.

[22] A.B. Simpson, *The Alliance Weekly*, Dec. 30, 1919, p. 212.

[23] Boardman, *The Higher Christian Life*, pp. 153-154.

[24] The words of this hymn by Simpson were sometimes misconstrued with the "Oneness" sect led by Frank Ewart, Glenn A. Cook and others, which J. Roswell Flowers opposed as leader of the Assemblies of God. The Oneness sect with its unitarian position was organized as the Apostolic Assemblies in 1917.

[25] Pardington, *The Crisis of the Deeper Life*, p. 177.

6
Sanctification and "Spirit-Corporeity"

The Alliance was dominated by a particular worldview that envisioned Christ as sovereign in authority and power over heaven and earth, as Head of the church universal and as Lord of the harvest who would come again in great glory to establish His kingdom that now is advanced by the gospel.

The great mystery of the ages was stated in Colossians 1:27: "To them [the saints] God has chosen to make known among the Gentiles the glorious riches of this mystery, which is Christ in you, the hope of glory." The Alliance focused on the great truth that God had included man in a universal plan. Man can be justified, made a partaker of Christ's own nature through sanctifying grace and power and privileged to serve his Lord here and now for a kingdom that is eternal.

The phenomenal response the Alliance had from churches of various denominations to its vision of faith and challenge for missions began to change. From 1909, when Simpson was already past retiral age, until his death in 1919, the need for readjustment in the operation of the Alliance became increasingly apparent to its leaders. Yet, an original promise by the founder to cooperating churches was kept. The Alliance was not forming another church or denomination. But suddenly, and seemingly without anticipation, the evangelical world in which the Alliance was founded changed faster than Simpson could cope with in his usual masterful way.

The changes Simpson was facing related to the question as to what was the "real" or "true" church. In part, this was a by-product of the evangelical revival of 1857 which by the early 1900s was increasingly impacted by dispensational teaching on the spiritual nature of the church. The visible church was static to the evangelical mindset. It was loaded with historical baggage of clericalism, doctrinal and institutionalized rigidity and unresponsiveness to human need. The tendency to idealize the church by spiritualizing it and by-passing the visible church increased after the turn of the century. This seemingly made room for personal and lay involvement.

A theological fog shrouded the portion of the evangelical church interested in holiness. Partly this was due to the use of the phrase "the baptism of the Holy Ghost" with a wide divergence of meaning. Phoebe Palmer in the Wesleyan Holiness Movement in the 1860s, Boardman in the Higher Christian Life Movement by the 1870s, the Plymouth Brethren approach in the Keswick Movement by the 1880s, Simpson's projection in the Alliance movement by the 1890s and William Durham's interpretation in the Pentecostal movement by the 1900s each used the phrase. Yet each movement attached its own peculiar meaning to the term. This contributed to a confusion of issues regarding sanctification and the corporeity each particular interpretation produced.

Christ Himself, the Trinity and the Church

The Alliance interpretation of "the baptism of the Holy Spirit" focused mainly on Christ Himself. He Himself saved, sanctified and filled believers with the Holy Spirit. The centrality of Christ in Alliance teaching provided a thread of commonality with many evangelicals for a mutual understanding of the exaltation of Christ and its significance for world missions. But this was challenged by Pentecostalism with its fixation on speaking in tongues after the Asuza revival in 1906. It raised "the baptism of the Spirit" into a pneumatic issue that shook and realigned the evangelical world.

Between the "sleeping dogs" of mixed interpretation awakened by Pentecostalism on the issue of Spirit-baptism and the increasing threat of liberalism among the main denominations, now being divided by a form of dispensational-fundamentalism, the climate of evangelicalism changed dramatically.

The Alliance, with its emphasis on the Spirit-filled life, suffered heavy defection to Pentecostalism. Invitations for Bible and missionary conventions and the spawning of new branches tapered off as churches searched for their roots and built their defenses either for or against Pentecostalism or liberalism or both. In this critical situation the Alliance was challenged regarding its belief concerning Christ, the Trinity and the church.

The Alliance emphasis on the centrality of Christ was usually expressed in terms of "Christ Himself" or "Jesus Only" which outside its own familiar context sounded unitarian. Yet both Boardman and Simpson, who projected this emphasis to a large cross-section of evangelicals, held orthodox views of the Trinity. Boardman treated the Trinity extensively in Part II, chapter 1, in his first edition of *The Higher Christian Life* in 1859. Similarly, when Simpson presented *The Fourfold Gospel*, it was with a Trinitarian context.[1]

Concerning the triune God, Simpson warned of a subtle danger:

> . . . *that in our theological conception of the glorious Trinity that*

we sometimes make three gods instead of one. While there are three persons in the Godhead, yet there is one divine presence which the Holy Spirit brings to the heart and that is the presence of the Lord Jesus who is to us the Living Word and the one eternal Revelation of the Father.[2]

Simpson also clearly understood that the human nature of Jesus was not to be confused with His divine nature. The impartation of Christ's life did not make believers divine, but Christ's own nature was available to man because of the incarnation and the agency of the Holy Spirit. The very essence of the eternal life which Jesus came to secure for a lost world and which He described in His high-priestly prayer was "to know you, the only true God and Jesus Christ whom you have sent" (John 17:3).

To Simpson, the gospel of grace in Christ began with Genesis and climaxed with the book of Revelation. Jesus Christ was the main thread of divine revelation. The transition from the Old Covenant to the New came about when Jesus' humanity was glorified and He Himself sent the Holy Spirit to minister and reveal Him as Savior, Sanctifier, Healer and Coming King. The result was Pentecost and the New Testament church which is "the body of Christ" on earth. But the Old Testament saints were saved through the atonement Christ would yet provide, and the promises of Jeremiah 31:31-34 and Ezekiel 36:25-28 were fulfilled when Christ was glorified and the Holy Spirit was given.[3] In *The Fourfold Gospel*, Simpson asserts regarding Ezekiel 36:25:

. . . our whole being will be prompted by the springing life of God within. It is God manifest in flesh again. This is the only true consummation of sanctification. Thus only can man enter completely into the life of holiness. As we are thus possessed by the Holy Spirit we are made partakers of the Divine nature. It is a sacred thing for any man or woman to enter into this relation with God.[4]

In Simpson's theology this incarnational life of Christ is critical to a life of holiness and power. It was made available through Christ's life, death, resurrection and ascended glorification in fulfillment of Jeremiah 31 and Ezekiel 36. Yet, many believers have no "present" Christ, though they seek an experience of being filled with the Spirit as described in Acts 1:8. This is because they seek "the blessing" rather than "the Blesser," Christ Himself.

Henry Wilson, Simpson's closest associate, explains three views as to how Christ relates to believers—imitation, inspiration and incarnation. The first two in his view were partly true but inadequate in effectual power. Many believers have an abstract, theological Christ. Others have an historic, inspirational or ceremonial Christ. However, the vital force of the believer being in Christ and Christ in the believer, observed Wilson, displaces the agonizing, the straining and seeking for the Spirit's filling. With knowing Christ as Sanctifier comes a steady and quiet realization of full surrender that identifies with Christ Himself and claims the Spirit's filling He Himself provides.[5]

Christ promised to send the Holy Spirit as an afflatus to empower His followers for a unified witness to Himself. Only in the corporate sense can believers be witnesses in Jerusalem, Judea, Samaria and to the uttermost parts of the earth simultaneously. This witnessing power was to reach the whole world because of His incarnate work and glorification. It is through "his flesh" that the enmity of the ceremonial law was abolished and that Jew and Gentile are made "one new man" (Ephesians 2:14-15); it is through "his flesh" that believers become members of His body (Ephesians 5:29-30) and it is through "his flesh" that believers have access to God in prayer (Hebrews 10:20). Such incarnational work is presently made possible because the Spirit is the agent of the finished work of Christ.

The baptism of the Spirit referred to what was yet to come

at Pentecost. While the expression is used to describe the believer's spiritual entrance into the body of Christ (1 Corinthians 12:13), there remain aspects of the Pentecost event (Acts 1:8) that suggest new dimensions for Christian living and service not apparent in most churches. Hence the term "the baptism of the Spirit" seemed appropriate to Simpson.

Pentecost, in Alliance teaching, was more than an historic event. It was to make Christ presently available to believers personally and corporately.[6] As the cross is more than an historic event to believers who have personally identified with it, so Pentecost involves the availability of Christ's own life, His fullness and sufficiency for Christian living and serving. Simpson wrote:

> *The great mistake of the church has been the failure to recognize God's plan in ultimate and full perspective. Each event seen in proper relation to the others has an important bearing upon the whole, and the whole truth is necessary to rightly understand each part.*
>
> *The word* power *expresses the deep underlying truth that runs through the entire book of Acts. A supernatural person has come to indwell the bosom of the church. While Jesus is at the throne as head of the church, the power of the Holy Spirit is the heart of the church at work.*[7]

The Holy Spirit proceeds from the Father through the Son and does not act on His own. He comes into believers personally with corporate intentions to glorify and magnify Christ. However, Simpson believed, New Testament saints may live as Old Testament saints by not identifying with God's plan. This is why he spoke of the Holy Spirit being "with" believers in contrast to those indwelt by Christ personally and corporately through the baptism of the Spirit.[8]

The C&MA and the Dispensationalism in Keswick and Pentecostalism

Boardman and Simpson had a Christian life and worldview that did not admit the basic premise of J.N. Darby, the founder of dispensationalism. Darby was a lawyer who became a priest in the Church of England. As such he became hungry for spiritual reality. He came to understand that in the post-Pentecost economy, he was united to Christ in heaven by grace through faith. He concluded, therefore, that the heavenliness provided for the believer—which he had tried to achieve formerly in his old wretched "self"—was to be understood in contrast to the "law" of the Mosaic economy.

He drew a further distinction between the moral sins of Israel against Jehovah and the rejection of Christ as the Messiah in the Gospels. Consequently, there were two types of righteousness, the righteousness of the future kingdom (promised to David) for the Jews in the Old Testament saved under the law and the righteousness the church is privileged to receive from Christ under grace. Ultimately, according to Darby, the believing Jew of the Old Testament will inherit a kingdom on earth during the millennium as a reward for his type of righteousness, while the church that is raptured before the great tribulation receives a nobler reward, being with Christ in glory. At Pentecost, the economy of the Spirit superseded five previous economies in which man's failure and God's grace were progressively demonstrated. These previous economies disciplined man to discern the spiritual beyond the visible and material. The sixth economy, an age of the Spirit and of grace, was wholly spiritual and individualistic. The Holy Spirit now provided a dynamic of spirituality that was heavenly and not earthly; therefore the church of "Spirit-baptized" believers was not to be visualized or institutionalized with organizational membership.

However, the most critical claim of dispensationalism was that when the Jews rejected their Messiah, Christ's kingdom was postponed. This major premise artificially displaced Christ's power, authority and presence with that of the Holy Spirit. William L. Pettingill, a strong representative of the dispensational school, wrote:

> *I have long been convinced, and have taught that the Great Commission of Matthew 28:19, 20 is primarily applicable to the Kingdom rather than to the church. If this were kept in mind we should not fall into confusion regarding our marching orders, which are found in Acts 1:8, with details in the Epistles to the churches. The Matthew commission will come into force for the Jewish Remnant after the Church is caught away.*[9]

This teaching directly contradicted the "Christ Himself" teaching of Boardman and Simpson. It opened the door to a subjective spirituality expressed in Pentecostalism which one historian analyzes as a direct result of dispensationalism.[10]

Sanctification, the Baptism of the Spirit and the Church

In Simpson's interpretation of Spirit-baptism, the church's moral and equipping aspects coincided with knowing Christ as Sanctifier. Christ Himself produces a personal and corporate effectiveness for the world-wide witnessing He promised in Acts 1:8. Sanctification and equipping for service reflected the holiness and authority of Christ Himself who indwells His people by the Spirit.[11] It was from this vantage point that Simpson envisioned a "Spirit-baptized" corporeity in the Alliance. But again, he was not thinking of organized or visible churches, *per se*, but of people within visible churches who were bonded by prayer and involvement in Christ's great commission.

The "branch-strategy" of the Alliance was ruled by an expediency that fitted the mindset of evangelicalism in his day, particularly the dispensational view of the church. Though Simpson had very definite views on the visible, local church which were not in accord with dispensational teaching, he considered the neglect of missions by existing churches and the needs of the world more important than disputation over the doctrine of the church. What was not realized by Simpson or by evangelicals at large was that Darby's view of the church was a key factor in the dispensationalist interpretation of Christology and pneumatology.

Changes of structure in the early Alliance and changes of Alliance self-expression can best be perceived with this understanding. But at the core of Alliance existence was its view of sanctification and the baptism of the Spirit to fulfill the Great Commission. Christ Himself has the right, the privilege and the power to fulfill the world mandate, and this the Alliance wished to share in branch forms of corporeity. These were to work in and with the churches and not independently of them.

Sanctification and "Spirit-baptized" Corporeity in Transition

The Alliance believed it was marshaling neglected forces in existing churches, mobilizing them with a message that was mostly neglected and fulfilling the neglected duty of missions for the church at large. Simpson wanted the Alliance to vitalize and complement the church, not to divide it with nonessential issues. He had a profound respect for the visibly organized church and believed that it should reflect a biblical pattern in which the intrinsic and extrinsic were integrated. However, this would only happen as the church embraced a vision for missions and believers were filled with the Holy

Spirit. He described this filling as a definite experience:

> *There is a moment in which we actually enter into personal
> union with Jesus and receive the baptism of the Holy Ghost. In
> that moment we are fully accepted and are fully sanctified up to
> all the light we have. But as light grows deeper and clearer He
> leads us farther down, and farther on, at once revealing and heal-
> ing every secret thing that is contrary to His perfect will, as we are
> able to bear it, and bringing us into perfect conformity to the very
> nature and life of Christ.*[12]

No doubt the Alliance leaders were aware that the Alliance
was vulnerable to change because of the various interpretations
of sanctification and "the baptism of the Holy Spirit," but
they considered the Alliance could work with existing churches without being divisive because Christ Himself was the Great
Reconciler. Simpson warned the Alliance constituency frequently that to bring any division to the existing churches
was a heinous sin directly contrary to the purpose of the
Alliance. There was something incarnational about the visible
church that was not to be violated. Consequently, marked
changes in historical development in the functional operation
of the Alliance occurred.

Transitional Changes in the
Visible Expression of Alliance Fellowship

From 1887 to 1907: The Christian Alliance emerged out of
Bible and missionary conventions. The model for a missionary
convention came out of the New York Gospel Tabernacle. It
was exported after 1885 to large metropolitan areas through a
description in *The Word, the Work and the World.* The Tabernacle
model as a missionary church became an important reference for the deeper life message and a missionary appeal in
various churches. The magazine regularly featured "The Taber-

nacle Pulpit" and news items of activities in the Tabernacle, along with selected features of convention work and the various results. It gave large emphasis to the missionary efforts of all agencies and the progress being made in world-wide missions. Branches were generated from the Bible and missionary conventions. They grew out of a deeper life message that was presented in eight to 10 days of preaching with an emphasis on missions in the last several days. Interested people who committed themselves to the Alliance message and vision for missions were given opportunity for its support and were invited to an informal membership in a branch. Here missionaries on furlough would minister along with other leaders of the Alliance and people would fellowship in the support of the Christian Alliance under the guidance of a local superintendent. Such activities were not to interfere with the normal activities of the regular churches.

Simpson believed that Alliance people would be the most supportive members in their churches as well as in the Alliance. The most significant issue was not missions, *per se*, but the sanctification of the members in relation to the Head of the church and the Lord of the harvest. Non-essential doctrinal issues were mute questions. Overt controversy between Arminianism and Calvinism was avoided.

During this 20-year period, the Alliance experienced phenomenal growth to about 300 local organizations and 300 missionaries by 1907. It was only restricted by its capacity to meet demands. Its acceptance in evangelical churches was somewhat comparable to that of the Billy Graham Association in our day. The evangelical climate reflected the revival of 1857-1858 from which many parachurch agencies emerged— missionary societies, Bible societies, the Moody Evangelistic Association, the Student Volunteer movement, the Y.M.C.A., the Sunday School movement, etc. Dispensationalism contributed strongly to interdenominationalism and the methods used in parachurch operations after 1890. That the dispensational doctrine of the church was the catalytic agent for its other teachings should not be overlooked.[13] That the true church was spiritual, that it was born from above to exist in the heavenlies and outside of history and that it had a "spiritual" corporeity was increasingly emphasized as liberalism cast its ever-widening influence. The institutional church was often portrayed by dispensational leaders as a necessary evil in parallel to liberal churches which relied heavily on organization and membership.

W.E. Blackstone, who rallied people at Old Orchard for the formation of an Alliance in 1886 wrote in his very popular book *Jesus Is Coming,* "There is truly a church, and it is the body of Christ, ONE AND INDIVISIBLE, composed of all true believers in Him. It may be called a church within, or among the churches,—the wheat among the chaff."[14] He believed that the birds of the air and the leaven depicted in the parables of Matthew 13, represented the members who lodged in the visible church that was merely formal and nominal.[15] George Marsden has observed:

> *American dispensationalists thought of religion primarily in terms of individuals rather than institutions. The important spiritual unit was the individual. The church existed as a body of sanctified individuals united by commitment to Christ and secondarily as a network of ad hoc spiritual organizations. The institutional church hence had no particular status.*[16]

While dispensational emphases did not basically change Alliance doctrine, their influence affected the function of the C&MA in its initial growth and by the 1920s their popularity often confused Alliance teaching on sanctification and the church. Furthermore, Simpson's "Spirit-baptized" fraternal fellowship, which was to marshal the neglected lay forces in the churches for world evangelization experienced a severe setback from the Pentecostal assault that came between 1906 and 1908 with its version of "Spirit-baptism." It is doubtful that there was anything more shocking and more trying to Simpson's entire ministry. The teaching of Pentecostalism seemingly produced a divide and conquer strategy and an elitism that denied accommodation. The tongues evidence theory excluded all who denied this doctrinal position.

From 1908 to 1919: Pentecostalism caused a dramatic realignment of existing churches particularly among the churches that espoused holiness. The Wesleyan Holiness movement denounced Pentecostalism in 1912. Early Keswick-dispensationalism was reshaped by the initiation of an "American Keswick" in 1913 by Charles G. Trumbull to emphasize "victorious living." Pentecostal-Holiness churches separated from the Assemblies of God when it was organized in 1914. By 1907, no less than 25 different Holiness denominations had developed, and most aligned themselves for or against the tongues-evidence doctrine.

The result was that denominational churches with whom the Alliance had been working cooperatively tended to become protective and defensive. Not only was "Spirit-baptism" suspect in whatever way it was expressed, but, in addition, the creeping inroads of liberalism began to occupy the attention of evangelical churches. Many churches began to rearrange their loyalties; battle-lines were frequently drawn between congregations and their denomination. The Fundamentalist Association (strongly dispensational) was organized in 1919, and its manner of confrontation with liberalism often divided churches. These changes strongly affected the Alliance in this period.

World War I also affected the Alliance between 1914 and 1918. Convention work was curtailed with travel restrictions and, with it, the beginning of new branches. The Alliance reported approximately the same number of organized branches supporting the same number of missionaries in 1919 as in 1907. In the meantime, the Alliance reorganized in 1912, and at the 1914 Council, Simpson projected 10 statements to solidify the identity of the Alliance. The climate for an interdenominational, "Spirit-baptized" fellowship no longer prevailed. Clearly the Alliance needed a more practical form of identity. The founder's ministry finished its course when he died in 1919.

From 1920 to 1940: No single person affected the Alliance more strongly after Simpson's death than Paul Rader who succeeded him as president. His theology was initially nurtured under E.D. "Daddy" Whiteside in Pittsburg and the great missionary conventions in Carnegie Hall, as well as under the ministry of Simpson at Old Orchard. His most obvious gift was evangelism, and evangelism was aggressively practiced in the C&MA in rescue missions, neglected rural areas, mountain mining towns or union meetings with cooperating churches. The branches, however, existed mostly in urban areas and were designed to promote the support of missions and to cultivate deeper life fellowship among believers of various churches. They were not designed for evangelism and discipleship of new members.

For the Alliance to carry on "branch-evangelism" and to cultivate discipleship with responsible membership misrepresented their established design. Between 1912 to 1916 Simpson strongly urged His constituents to observe the design of the branch. The ordinances were not to be observed and the informal members of the Alliance were to be members in good standing in other churches.

When Bible and missionary convention work waned because of the war, Pentecostalism and the inroads of liberalism, so did the branches. No doubt, Simpson before his death, as well as Rader after him, realized that change was inevitable if the

Alliance was to survive. Perhaps Simpson perceived new hope for the Alliance in Rader's dynamic evangelistic capacity if it could somehow be incorporated with the Alliance branch concept.

After Rader became pastor of Moody Church in 1914, a large tabernacle seating 5,000 was erected to promote evangelism—Billy Sunday style. It was intended to stand for three months but stayed up for 10 years, and for a number of years evangelistic services were held six nights a week with many conversions. Several years before Rader became president of the C&MA in 1919, he was commissioned by the Board of Managers to spearhead what was called "The Forward Movement." This was an effort to involve churches of various denominations in mass evangelistic crusades and to incorporate a deeper life and missionary emphasis.

It is possible, as some have thought, that Simpson coveted Rader as pastor of the New York Gospel Tabernacle to supply a fresh thrust for evangelism in a regular church. When offered the opportunity after Simpson's death, Rader refused and remained pastor at Moody Church for two years while president of the C&MA. Rader's vision, as realized later by Alliance leaders, was to catapult the home work of the Alliance into mass evangelism and to absorb the branches into "Tabernacle Commissions" that would promote evangelism and missions. The commissions that programmed tabernacle activities were made up of selected individuals and were self-perpetuating in that they would elect members to their commission as needed. Rader envisioned that these tabernacles would eventually absorb the branches.

Eventually, four teams were formed under Rader's leadership to forward the Tabernacle movement after he resigned from Moody Church in 1921. Mass crusades were held across the United States and Canada attracting thousands in the larger metropolitan areas. The post World War I era was ripe for mass evangelism. Tabernacles with sawdust floors, plank benches and large platforms were built. Accommodations were arranged for branch meetings in conjunction with the tabernacle commissions. Rader viewed this as an accommodation in transition. Tabernacles represented a new "Spirit-baptized" corporeity that reflected a dispensational theology of the church—Rader style. This to him was the parenthetical church awaiting the rapture.

Despite the phenomenal success of "tabernacleism," these developments caused the old guardians of Alliance heritage to become more and more apprehensive. But Rader took no orders from headquarters or an institutionalized organization. He managed programs and finances so compulsively that his removal as president of the C&MA became inevitable. It occured in 1924, but the Alliance was forever changed.

From 1924 to 1940, through the depression and the approach of World War II, the Alliance struggled on, seeking its own "Spirit-baptized" corporeity. When Frederick Senft became president in 1924, he represented much of the original spirit of the Alliance. He had served the Alliance branch in Philadelphia for 28 years where there was a large tabernacle and where the program was conducted much in the style of the New York Gospel Tabernacle. Through Senft, together with E.J. Richards, the home secretary, a suggested constitution for affiliated churches patterned after the New York Gospel Tabernacle was adopted by Council. Ostensibly, the branches would remain under the old branch constitutions, but most adopted the provisions of the suggested constitution designed to preserve the tabernacles for the support of the Alliance.

The Indigenous Church and Alliance Identity

From 1941 to 1971: It is difficult to analyze what becomes more nearly contemporary, but history will no doubt record that what was happening in Alliance missionary operations affected the "Spirit-corporeity" of Alliance fellowship at home. World War II brought an end to the old colonial empires. Indigenous churches that would be self-governing, self-supporting and self-propagating became an urgent necessity.

Previously, missionary operations depended on missionary control rather than upon the church as God's incarnational agency that should multiply and grow responsibly with accountability. Though an indigenous concept was projected when the Alliance was founded in 1887, the evangelical and world climate militated against it. The colonial mentality pervaded missionary efforts and this was conveniently accommodated particularly by the fundamentalist-dispensational mindset regarding the church.

In 1955 the Alliance Council mandated the implementation of indigenous church operations by 1960 in all its fields. However, this held direct implications for Alliance fellowships at home as their counterpart, though the C&MA still called itself an interdenominational missionary society. The church in a biblical sense is the church at home or overseas and must indigenously accept its complete responsibility and accountability.

By 1965, a formal statement of doctrine was adopted. Its statement on sanctification was adopted as follows:

> *It is the will of God that each believer be filled with the Holy Spirit and be sanctified wholly, being separated from sin and the world and fully dedicated to the will of God, thereby receiving power for holy living and effective service. This is both a crisis and a progressive experience wrought in the life of the believer subsequent to conversion.*

Neither in Scripture nor in the practice of the Alliance is "sanctified wholly" (1 Thessalonians 5:23) viewed as classifying saints; rather, it is a divine calling and the only norm for effective Christian living and dynamic church life.

By 1971, reorganization was effected that would reflect the character of an indigenous church at home. In the meantime, the church-growth movement influenced the Alliance to promote evangelism and to plant new churches; that has greatly affected its nature and function as a denomination of churches.

From 1972 to the present: The pressing issue of our time is to recognize how the legacy of the Alliance is to be preserved in the midst of so much change that is accelerating even now. The doctrinal issue of sanctification that was so crucial to the formation and development of the Alliance is still crucial. New and pressing questions emerge: How is "Spirit-corporeity" in the Alliance to be realized? How can the deeper life and missions emphases be promoted on biblical grounds that preserve the historical and theological integrity of the Alliance? Such questions cannot be ignored and presently require urgent attention.

FOOTNOTES

[1] A.B. Simpson, *The Fourfold Gospel,* pp. 100-103.

[2] A.B. Simpson, *When the Comforter Came,* (Harrisburg: Christian Publications, Inc., 1911), Day one of a daily devotional.

[3] A.B. Simpson, *The Holy Spirit or Power From on High,* Vol. 1, (Harrisburg: Christian Publications, Inc., n.d.), pp. 226-228, 240-241.

[4] A.B. Simpson, *The Fourfold Gospel,* p. 40.

[5] Henry Wilson, *The Internal Christ,* (NY: The Christian Alliance Press, 1902), pp. 12, 42-45.

[6] A.B. Simpson, *The Holy Spirit,* Vol 2, (Harrisburg: Christian Publications, Inc., n.d.), p. 19.

[7] A.B. Simpson, *The Spirit-Filled Church in Action,* (Vol. 16 of Christ in the Bible Series) (Harrisburg: Christian Publica-

tions, Inc., reprint 1975), p. 30.

[8] "Some Aspects of the Holy Spirit" in *Living Truths*, Sept. 1906, p. 523. See also—editorial, *Living Truths*, March, 1906, p. 130.

[9] William L. Pettingill, *Bible Questions Answered*, (Findlay, OH: Fundamental Truth Publishers, n.d.), p. 112.

[10] Robert Mabes Anderson, *Vision of the Disinherited—The making of American Pentecostalism*, p. 43. Anderson writes: "The Keswick movement as we shall see, was absolutely necessary to the development of Pentecostalism. . . . that wing of the Pentecostal movement which had earlier connections with Wesleyanism became Pentecostal by accepting Keswick teaching on dispensationalism, . . ." Simpson observed: "We believe that the Alliance teaching on this subject (sanctification) is neither Wesleyan nor an echo of the excellent teaching given at Keswick. . . . There is always a little danger of seeing our experiences more than seeing the source of that experience, the Lord Jesus. We have been led to rise above all our experiences and recognize our resurrection life as wholly in Him." (Editorial, *The C&MA*, January, 1899. p. 8).

[11] A.B. Simpson, *The Spirit-Filled Church in Action*, p. 12.

[12] A.B. Simpson, *The Holy Spirit*, Vol. 2, pp. 229-230.

[13] Earnest Sandeen expresses the belief that Darby's doctrine of the church was the catalytic agent for the rest of his beliefs. *The Roots of Fundamentalism*, p. 66.

[14] William E. Blackstone, *Jesus is Coming*, (NY: Fleming H. Revell Co., 1908), p. 95.

[15] Ibid.

[16] George E. Marsden, *Fundamentalism and American Culture*, p. 71.

7
Sanctification and the Corporate Church

P ardington in *Outline Studies in Christian Doctrine* clearly sets forth Alliance teaching on the local church as "a body of professed believers, baptized on a credible confession of faith in Him, and associated for worship, work, and discipline" and also as "a company of believers called out from the world, voluntarily joined together and meeting at stated times, among whom the Word of God is preached, discipline is administered, and the ordinances observed."[1] However, the doctrine of the church was only indirectly relevant to the C&MA because it was an organization of branches, not churches, as long as Simpson lived.

Simpson clearly distinguished branches from regular churches such as the New York Gospel Tabernacle. He described the branches as being "irregular." Furthermore, in spite of the mainstream evangelical mindset regarding the church and the poorly developed ecclesiology in Protestant thought of that day,[2] Simpson had a remarkably strong conviction of the nature and function of the structured church. He wrote:

This house has a divine pattern. Just as the tabernacle of old was to be constructed strictly according to the pattern that was shown

103

to Moses on the Mount, so the Church of Christ has a divine plan
and should be in every particular constructed accordingly. The
failure to do this has been the cause of all the apostasies, declen-
sions, and mistakes of the past eighteen centuries. It is the reason
why the heathen world is still lying in darkness and crying to God
against the unfaithfulness of His people.[3]

The Church and the Need for Sanctification

Our day of sudden change needs both theology and an
historical perspective. Where an historical understanding is
least real, the theological understanding is most empty. Since
the New Testament Church has been nurtured by the Word of
Christ and the Holy Spirit has taught faithful members a history of theology must be taken seriously as a heritage left to us
for instruction. If we do not know where we have come from,
we do not know where we are or where we are going.

This, however, does not mean that we are enslaved by a past
we dare not change. Change is inevitable and the present is
meant to benefit from the past. But it must be done with a
sense of continuity in the midst of change. The seven churches in Revelation 2 and 3 were urged to search out their particular roots and to trace God's hand of providence and discipline. To the church of Ephesus the warning was given
"Remember the height from which you have fallen! Repent
and do the things you did at first. If you do not repent, I will
come to you and remove your lampstand from its place" (2:5).

An understanding of Alliance history reveals the necessity for
change. But this change must be conditioned by a more complete understanding of a sanctified people with a "Spirit-corporeity"; how this is to represent a lampstand in which Christ's
presence is manifest. Simpson often reminded Alliance constituents of the need for God's providential correction "to
our particular sphere of service and the organized work which

God has given us as a peculiar trust, and yet to the larger fellowship of the whole body of Christ."[4] He spoke directly against those who spoke of the Holy Spirit in a utilitarian sense as "power for service." They seemingly failed to comprehend the need to identify with Christ as Sanctifier and a sanctified community. Commenting on Matthew 12:28. "But if I drive out demons by the Spirit of God, then the kingdom of God has come upon you" he said:

> *That is to say, it is the Holy Ghost that casts out demons in us, and this same Holy Ghost is to remain in us and to perpetuate the Kingdom of God in the church through this dispensation.*
>
> *It is the very wonderful truth that it is the same Spirit who wrought in Christ, that He has given to the church to perform her work of love and power. This is what the Master meant when He said, "He that believeth on me, the works that I do shall he do because I go unto the Father." The Holy Ghost in us is the same Holy Ghost that wrought in Christ.*[5]

Simpson explains that Christ wanted His followers to know that His miracles and power as Son of Man were not by His inherent power but a power that dwelt in Him; therefore the kingdom of God had come nigh to them. This would not be withdrawn by His return to heaven but instead would be made available to them to carry on the same ministry He had begun. Christ has received a kingdom power that through His incarnation and finished work is to be realized through His church by the Holy Spirit. In other words, the same Spirit that indwells Him and proceeds from Him now indwells the church.

Referring to Acts 1:8—"But you will receive power when the Holy Spirit comes on you; and you will be my witnesses in Jerusalem, and in all Judea and Samaria, and to the ends of the earth"—Simpson emphasized that this was primarily the power "to be," not merely the power to say and do. Their "being" was to be a witness to Christ. "Our service and testimony will be the outcome of our life and experience. . . . Nothing is so strong as the influence of a consistent, supernatural, and holy character."[6]

Time and again, Simpson revealed a reaction against an emphasis upon "power for service" to the neglect of "power for being." In an editorial he criticized the Wesleyan and Keswick holiness movements for not emphasizing the source of their holiness and power as wholly in Christ. He exhorted Alliance constituents to "maintain an attitude of consistent dependence every moment on our union and communion with Him."[7] While empowering for service was an important dimension for this age, to Simpson it was a secondary one. The principle task of the Holy Spirit was to present Christ in His fullness and sufficiency and to impart the benefits of union with Him to believers in communal body-life. The Holy Spirit was given to the Church on the day of Pentecost to help them embody Christ to the world, not in any way to glorify man or to magnify individual achievement.

In our present culture the emphases on personal fulfill-ment and individual rights almost preclude responsibilities of family life. Instead of the individual serving the family, the fam-ily is expected to be at the service of the individual. We live in a "divorce culture"—"If you don't meet my needs, sweetheart, I am splitting." But marriage as it is instituted of God involves total self-giving to make marriage and the family what it should be. Similarily, the church is instituted of God on a self-giving basis: "Husbands, love your wives, just as Christ loved the church and gave himself up for her to make her holy" (Eph-esians 5:25).

The problems of the family and of the church tend to coin-cide. A lack of understanding of what it means to be a member of Christ's body, sanctified and meet for the Master's use, eventually determines the church's character. Today, the Alliance needs its message of sanctification as never before. It is one thing through branch-structure to complement existing churches with the message of "Christ as Sanctifier" along with the intent of promoting a missionary society, but it is another to demonstrate what the church is designed to be in corporate nature and function.

Sanctification and the Design of the Church

Alliance theology clearly suggests that sanctification is necessary to the design of the church. It involves every member because what the members are determines what the church is. The congregation is the interpreting context for the gospel preached and the primary base for world evangelization. The privilege and duty of every Christian is to receive Christ as Sanctifier and the Holy Spirit by a conscious, definite act of appropriating faith just as truly as he has initially received Christ as Savior. It is through this kind of relationship that God's purpose in the church will be realized.

In his annual report to Council in 1980, President Louis L. King concluded with these words:

> *While in the process of time the society aspect of the Alliance has gradually emerged into a denomination, the particular and special purpose of the organization remains the same. Instead of being a society of believers fellowshipping around a message and a mission, we are now a church with the same message and the same mission. Only the organizational structure has changed. The purpose remains constant.*[8]

Perhaps in an effort to emphasize continuity and to minimize change, we are in danger of overlooking the significant changes the Alliance is experiencing from being an interdenominational missionary society at the turn of the 20th century to becoming a denomination of churches at the turn of the 21st century. For this, we need an updated vision with a fresh anointing of God's Spirit because historical overhang can blind us.

Formerly, the Alliance rode an evangelical wave at its crest and its Christ-centered message of sanctification reverberated harmoniously with a sounding-board of cross-denominational churches. But in the period between 1909 to 1919 the evangelical world changed dramatically as already observed. However, in the latter half of the 20th century, at a time when the Alliance reorganized into a denomination of churches, the evangelical church was dislocated from its Constantinian-like culture and entered a post-Christian era. In fact, the church is now under siege by a secular culture that accepts science and technology as "truth" and makes economic success autonomous.

The church's former perception of missions was "foreign missions" or "overseas missions." Today, the third world is more responsive to the gospel than the Western world and the church must be missionary at home to survive. It now has two fronts not only because of its dislocated function in culture but because ethnic immigration has brought third world missions to its very doorstep. Missions, therefore, has lost its simplistic focus and has no cultural home base.

Furthermore, for the Alliance to function as a denomination rather than a society makes a difference as to how evangelism and discipleship is fostered, what function worship has, how lay leaders and ministerial leaders are trained and equipped, how families, singles and youth are ministered to, etc. But of paramount importance to an Alliance doctrine of the church is how the message of sanctification and missions is made relevant to the total nature and function of the church. The current crisis has to do with the way an Alliance church sees itself and forms its life.

The heritage of Alliance purpose will best be preserved when it is seen in a full and ultimate perspective as to what the

New Testament pattern for the church demands. If properly designed spiritually and physically, Simpson believed that "all the apostasies, declensions and mistakes" experienced in the previous 18 centuries could be avoided and the heathen world would no longer lay in darkness and despair without the gospel. This is the challenge the Alliance now confronts if the founder's idealism for the church is biblically true.

The simplicity often expressed in a call for revival or for supernatural signs and wonders is not a likely answer if the spiritual and physical design of the church is impractical and unbiblical. Speaking about the need for signs and wonders as described of the early church, Simpson declared:

> *We are not to go abroad to preach the signs, nor to begin with the signs, nor to produce the signs ourselves. Our business is not to work miracles and wait until we can do so before telling the story of Jesus. Our work is to tell the simple story of His life and death and His resurrection and to preach the Gospel in its purity. But we do it expecting the Lord to prove the reality of His power, and to give the signs He has promised.*
>
> *Now, in order to do this, there must not only be faith on the part of the isolated missionary, but there must be supporting faith on the part of those who send him. There must be the united expectancy of the missionary abroad and the church at home, reaching across and around the world, and touching heaven with a chain of believing prayer. We must more and more recognize this if we expect our missionaries to be armed with a special supernatural power, and our work abroad to have the very same features as the work at home. Too little have we recognized this, but as we do so more and more, God will meet our expectation.*[9]

The convictions of the founder of the C&MA regarding the church at home or the missionary overseas, regarding the centrality of the gospel in its purity, regarding the relation of the sending church to missionaries and the need to recognize this more and more, has its greatest challenge for us today as a denomination of churches.

Since the indigenous church policy was put in place in 1960, Alliance churches overseas have more than doubled each decade since then, so that nearly 12,000 organized ("Alliance") churches now exist in about 50 countries. To be a missionary church that carries the message of the gospel in its purity and with a proper design of the church is the challenge.

Alliance researcher and writer, Samuel Wilson, wrote: "The Gospel is near meaningless in hermitage. The kind of living community that helps me discover the Gospel's meaning is, according to Christ, the credential of the church to the world. . . . Only as churches are planted in a people group is there any possibility of producing a Gospel movement capable of evangelizing."[10] The message of Christ as Sanctifier is contagious in community. The credentials of a church before the world are established not only by its proclamation but by its demonstrated quality of fellowship in which union with Christ is lived out in flesh and blood reality.

In the loose structure of the branch and as a missionary society of the C&MA, sanctification was commonly perceived in terms of individualism rather than communal discipleship. Sanctification should be communicated in communal life because holiness will inevitably be expressed relationally. This becomes the basis for all effective service to Christ. Dr. A.W. Tozer observed:

> *The popular notion that the first obligation of the church is to spread the gospel to the uttermost parts of the world is false. Her first obligation is to be spiritually worthy to spread it. Our Lord said, "Go ye," but He also said, "Tarry ye," and the tarrying had to come before the going. Had the disciples gone forth as missionaries before the day of Pentecost it would have been an overwhelming spiritual disaster, for they could have done no more than make converts after their own likeness, and this would*

*have altered for the worse the whole history of the Western world
and had consequences throughout the ages to come.*[11]

From its initial beginning as a society the Alliance recognized that the deeper life was fundamental to its missionary cause. How this applies to the Alliance as a missionary church is an important issue. Some say the missionary dimension of the Alliance is being displaced, and the Alliance as a denomination is concerned about self-preservation. This must be analyzed primarily in terms of what sanctification means for the function of the church as a whole.

The Church and Sanctification in Function

The Scriptures describe believers in the church as growing in two ways—centripetally (inward growth) and centrifugally (outward growth). Believers are to grow up "into Christ" for maturity because infants without growth become tragic. Stead-

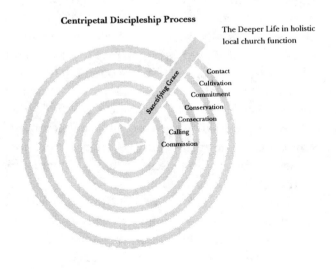

Centripetal Discipleship Process

The Deeper Life in holistic
local church function

Sanctifying Grace

Contact
Cultivation
Commitment
Conservation
Consecration
Calling
Commission

fastness in doctrine is to mark the church's maturity. "Then we will no longer be infants, tossed back and forth by the waves, and blown here and there by every wind of teaching . . . Instead, speaking the truth in love, we will in all things grow up into him who is the Head, that is, Christ"(Ephesians 4:14-15). The seven steps of growth (see illustration on p. 111) which sanctifying grace produces should lead to a complete identification with Christ and His kingdom work. Though uniform growth in definite stages is not realistic to real life, each step in continuous function will ideally be true in the spiritual life of a growing church.

The Scriptures assume that sound doctrinal teaching in the spirit of love will produce a steady spiritual growth process in the life of the church. This was notably true during Simpson's ministry in the New York Gospel Tabernacle. The seven converging points on the spiral lines suggest the kind of spiritual development the centripetal process of discipleship a growing church may have if it truly believes in the deeper life or sanctification. When the centrality of Christ is being modeled by pastors, elders and church leaders, the unsaved are contacted, cultivated and brought to conversion and commitment to Christ. These will also be conserved for responsible membership. As members of Christ's body, they observe baptism and communion. This was also exemplified in the New York Gospel Tabernacle where evangelism was not manufactured but was a well-spring of the congregation. Members were added by baptism and discipled through the training ministry of the church by normal process.

It is of interest at this point that Simpson's view of baptism included more than initial conversion. He said: "The ordinance of baptism, while initiatory of the Christian church, looks forward to entire sanctification and reaches its full significance only in complete death with Jesus Christ to self and sin." He believed that baptism should be performed with this understanding.[12]

The believer should immediately be led to consecration by accepting Christ as Sanctifier and by appropriating the filling of the Spirit. The result would be that the believer's gifts would be anointed of the Spirit with a calling to service, and every believer would be as ready to obey the Great Commission as the ones who actually are called to be missionaries. The lay member in secular vocations is as necessary to the church's total function as those in church vocations and will be equally rewarded for his faithfulness.

It is easy to recognize that in Simpson's concept of the church, if the model illustrated by the spiral holds true, that sanctification belongs to the heart of it. Everything focuses on the centrality of Christ and union with Him. Evangelism is not an end in itself; it is always for Christ's sanctifying work and the church's ministry to reach the world for Christ.

The church is also to go out (centrifugally) and radiate the gospel to the world. The Great Commission was given on the basis of Christ's authority, power and presence in disciple-making. Simultaneously then (imposing the centrifugal on the centripetal), the purpose of the church is "to fill all things," as the Apostle Paul states in Ephesians 4:10 (KJV). He further describes this in 1:22-23 of the same epistle: "And God placed all things under his feet and appointed him to be head over everything for the church, which is his body, the fullness of him who fills everything in every way." The Alliance has always believed that only a global goal adequately expresses Christ's sovereign power and authority. To be in union with Christ's sanctifying power should make the church effectively missionary.

To bring the goal of missions to pass, worship must necessarily be central because the centrality of Christ demands it. Prayer, confession, praise and the ministry of the Word led by those commissioned for leadership is vital in worship. The

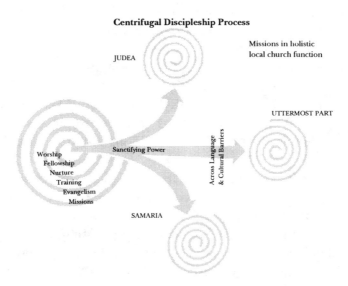

Centrifugal Discipleship Process

JUDEA

Missions in holistic
local church function

UTTERMOST PART

Sanctifying Power

Worship
Fellowship
Nurture
Training
Evangelism
Missions

Across Language
& Cultural Barriers

SAMARIA

assembly of God's people and their relatedness to God and to
each other is to unite them in worship, develop fellowship and
the affirmation of their faith. Their spiritual gifts will complement each other in their mutual concern and vision. It is in
worship that communal body-life is shaped and molded, where
the cost of discipleship is recognized with a willingness to pay
the price.

Through nurture and training members are equipped for
service. "Teaching them to obey everything I have com-
manded" is a large order that should result in motivating
evangelism and missions.

Personal sanctification, then, finds its highest meaning and
sense of fulfillment in responsibility through corporate sanctification, especially as the church expresses itself in world
mission.

A hymn written by the founder enforces this truth:

We are going forth from the school of Jesus,
We have sat at His blessed feet,
We have drunk from truth's celestial fountain,
We have tasted its honey sweet.
We are witnesses for our blessed Master,
In a world where friends are few,
And He sends us forth with the watchword holy,
Whatsoever it costs, be true.[13]

Corporate sanctification is not communal sanctification. The church only reflects sanctifying grace as individual believers know and experience Christ as their Sanctifier and become accountable to the body and to leadership that proclaims and models Christ Himself. However, when this is happening within the church, sanctifying grace becomes contagious and inspires the out-moving life of the church.

The Moravians had a motto: "The light that shines farthest shines brightest nearest home." When vibrant sanctifying grace is experienced in the heart-core of the church, the rest of its members and adherents will taste truth's celestial fountain and its honey sweet. A missionary church without a message of sanctification is virtually impossible because its energy base will be weak and uncertain. For this reason Simpson felt strongly that a home base committed to the deeper life was essential for the missionary task; also, as Simpson believed, the missionary work of the Alliance needs to be accountable to a body of Christians who hold the same truth in mutual trust.

To see the church in ultimate and full perspective provides a context for the meaning of personal sanctification. It reinforces the need for the deeper life and for missions which the Alliance believed so strongly in its early beginnings.

The Church and Sanctification in Balanced Perspective

The message of sanctification is not an exclusive message. The Alliance projected it in the content of an emphasis upon

Christ as Savior, Sanctifier, Healer and Coming King. Naturally, preaching is to represent the whole counsel of God. The Apostle Paul could say with confidence that he was free of the blood of all men because he had not hesitated to proclaim the whole will of God (Acts 20:27). But the message of sanctification has had a distinctive quality from the beginning for the Alliance and its development. This has largely shaped its character and function. It held a crucial relationship to the whole nature of man, to the universal church of Jesus Christ and to the whole world.

A profound balance is to be recognized in the doctrine of sanctification itself. It is both personal and corporate. It is historically and presently objective as well as experientially true to life subjectively. Jesus Christ objectively manifested the Father in His incarnation and identified with us as Son of Man; He completely fulfilled the objective Word of God. But, He also sent the Holy Spirit to witness Christ's own life to us and to teach believers of His fullness and sufficiency subjectively. He is the only Mediator between God and man, the Man Christ Jesus. And, as there is balance in the atonement, there is balance also in its real-life application of inward growth and outward expression.

Though Christ's soon coming was considered by Simpson to be contingent on the gospel being given as a witness to the whole world, according to Matthew 24:14, His coming is also made contingent on the church being made holy, radiant and prepared for His coming (Ephesians 5:22-32). God desires His church to be radiantly attractive and Christ asserted the truth that if He would be lifted up, He would draw all men unto Himself (John 12:32). The church is God's instrument for this.

The C&MA was founded with these convictions, and today the inspiration of its legacy and a renewed vision of the truth of its heritage is needed. The conflict of the ages and the consummation are nearer now than when this expression of the faith was first developed. How the C&MA concludes its ministry is as important as its beginnings. Those who inherit the legacy of the Alliance need to pass its vision and inspiration to the next generation, and so on, until the Lord does appear.

The Scriptures depict the end times as climactic both in severe judgment and in glorious consummation. Those who are destined to experience these times have a special challenge and privilege to stand true for Christ and His kingdom. Even so come, Lord Jesus!

The second verse and chorus of the hymn quoted several pages earlier is as appropriate as it is significant:

Be True!
We are going forth, from the upper chamber,
From the days of our Pentecost,
We have given ourselves in a full surrender
And been filled with the Holy Ghost.
We are going forth as epistles holy
And to live as Christ would do,
Let us always represent our Master,
Let our life be always true.

Chorus:
Be true! Be true! Let the holy watchword ring;
Be true to your trust, Be true to your glorious King;
Be true! Be true! Whether friends be false or few;
Whatsoe'er betide, ever at His side, Let Him always find you true.[14]

The Church and Sanctification in Global Outreach

The potential of the corporate church locally and in cross-cultural outreach is not only expansive but explosive. The explosive power, however, depends on the balance developed between the visible and the invisible, the objective and the subjective. Ultimately, this must always be understood in terms of the centrality of Christ and the cross for the advancement of His kingdom.

The principle of synergism—in which the total effort and results are greater than the sum of the individual parts—reveals how union with Christ objectively and subjectively becomes an awesome combination. To know Christ as Sanctifier is an engaging faith, and a consecrated believer does not take sanctification for granted but cultivates it both personally and in community. His gifts are given to the believer to share with his brother and fruitfulness becomes an exhilarating quest. Every church has a corporate personality in the way the members reflect Christ to each other and to an outside world. Nothing is lost in the mix of contribution each one brings. What is there becomes more because each is amplified through the synergism of the body so that what was promised Moses becomes a truth in reality: "You will pursue your enemies . . . five of you will chase a hundred, and a hundred of you will chase ten thousand" (Leviticus 26:7-8).

The critical need for sanctification to be taught and cultivated can hardly be overestimated. It will affect a church's worship, fellowship, nurture, evangelism and missions. To be a stockholder in the corporate church of Jesus Christ has eternal dimensions and makes it an important investment house that requires intelligent watchfulness and involvement. The synergism for good may also be reversed for bad as Israel experienced, but the explosive synergism for good ought to train our vision, energize our intercessory prayer, solemnize our worship, enrich our fellowship, discipline our nurture, motivate our evangelism and sanctify the whole.

The Apostle Paul's worldview of the gospel stretches the comprehension of the mind:

> *I became a servant of this gospel by the gift of God's grace given me through the working of his power. Although I am less than the least of all God's people, this grace was given me: to preach to the*

Gentiles the unsearchable riches of Christ, and to make plain to everyone the administration of this mystery, which for ages past was kept hidden in God, who created all things. His intent was that now, through the church, the manifold wisdom of God should be made known to the rulers and authorities in the heavenly realms, according to his eternal purpose which he accomplished in Christ Jesus our Lord. (Ephesians 3:7-11)

The wide rationality with which Paul construed the church and the strategic position he assigned to its ministry is overwhelming. It is through the church that all of creation, including rulers and authorities in the heavenly realms, are to be confronted! It is through the church that the unsearchable riches of Christ are to be administered to everyone! One sees more clearly as to what directed and motivated Paul's ministry. It was God's eternal purpose in Christ and Paul lived and worked with this focus in mind without compromise or accommodation.

This, no doubt, was the mindset Christ expected of His disciples when He gave the great commission in Matthew 28:18-20, or in the promise He gave as recorded in Acts 1:8. We are disobedient if we deliberately dare to adjust our vision to anything less.

God's grace through the working of His power is as sufficient to fulfill the great commission in our day as it was in Paul's day. When the truth of sanctification is experienced personally and in the corporate life of the church, God's purpose for global evangelization will be realized. Our zeal for world evangelization will increase and frontiers will be reached. Our resources will be the unsearchable riches of Christ and not merely our institutions or improved wealth. All else we so desperately sense as needed will be supplied by the working of His power.

FOOTNOTES

[1] George P. Pardington, *Outline Studies in Christian Doctrine*, pp. 337-338.

[2] Theological writer Millard J. Erickson states that the reason there is such a lack of understanding of the basic nature of the church is that "at no point in the history of Christian thought has the doctrine of the church received the direct and complete attention which other doctrines have received." He quotes Colin W. Williams to say "little direct theological attention was ever given to the church itself probably because it was taken for granted." *Christian Theology*, Vol. 3, (Grand Rapids: Baker Book House, 1985), p. 1026.

[3] A.B. Simpson, *Missionary Messages*, (Harrisburg: Christian Publications, Inc., n.d.), p. 19.

[4] A.B. Simpson "The Fifteenth Annual Report," *The Christian and Missionary Alliance* (The Annual Survey of The C&MA by the president), p. 32.

[5] A.B. Simpson, *The Holy Spirit*, Vol. 2, p. 19.

[6] Ibid., pp. 79-80.

[7] A.B. Simpson, editorial, *The Christian and Missionary Alliance*, June 7, 1899, p. 8.

[8] The C&MA Ninety-third Annual Report for 1979 and Minutes of the General Council, Hartford, CT, May 13-18, 1980, p. 37.

[9] A.B. Simpson, *Missionary Messages*, pp. 29-30.

[10] Samuel Wilson, *Marc* publications of World Vision, March/April, 1983, p. 8-9.

[11] A.W. Tozer, editorial, *The Alliance Witness*, June 3, 1959, p. 2.

[12] A.B. Simpson, "Baptism and the Baptism of the Holy Spirit," *The Christian and Missionary Alliance*, May 17, 1902, p. 286.

[13] *Hymns of the Christian Life*, (Harrisburg: Christian Publications, Inc., 1978), p. 584.

[14] Ibid.

8
The Life of Sanctification

It is possible to put so much emphasis upon the entry level of the Spirit-filled life that the development of sanctification is neglected. In Alliance theology, Christ is perceived both as the model and the efficacious resource for normal Christian living. Christ Himself is the reality, substance and progenitor of the life He wants to reproduce in us by His Spirit.[1]

Through the cross we enter into a full and irrevocable identification with the Lord Jesus Christ. Subsequently, Christ's vicarious life becomes our vital life. This life is for everyone, even those who consider themselves least promising and most insignificant. The "Christ-life" is available to everyone equally. It is not reserved for special people or particular vocations, though it is most crucial for church leadership.

Sanctification and the Parallel of Christ's Relationship to the Holy Spirit

Simpson wrote: "This is a subject that is well worthy of the closest study, for it teaches us much practical truth, not only in connection with the Master but also with our own spiritual life.

For if He was our Forerunner, and if it be true that as He is, so are we also in this world, then the definite steps of our Lord's experience should be repeated and fulfilled in the lives of His followers."[2]

Christ's birth and early life was overshadowed by the Holy Spirit. He was born of the Spirit in human form sinless and so did not need to be "born again." Though as sinners we must be born again in order to become righteous, our righteousness in Christ is related to Christ's sinless life in His birth and earthly life. This happens in our justification.

"Yet," says Simpson, "there came a day when in some entirely new and higher sense the Holy Spirit, like a dove, descended and bode upon Him. From that time there were two personalities connected with the life and work of our Lord Jesus. The Son of God was in direct union with the Spirit of God and all His works were inspired by the Holy Ghost."[3]

Thus, Simpson asks, "Is it applying the parallel too rigidly to say that just as He was born of the Spirit and yet afterward was baptized of the Spirit in the sense of a direct personal union and indwelling of the Holy Ghost, so likewise His people should not only experience a new birth through the grace and power of the Holy Ghost, but should yield themselves, as He did in His baptism, for the indwelling and abiding of the Comforter in the very same sense in which the Spirit came to Him. There is no stronger argument for the spiritualness of this deeper experience which God is giving to so many of His children in these days than the example of the Master Himself."[4]

The baptism of the Spirit for Jesus then, was not a moral issue. It was a "learning of obedience" which exemplified a human and divine relationship that was vicarious in nature. Christ as Mediator also made this available to us by the cross on the day of Pentecost. There were no shortcuts to Jesus' identification with us. He entered into all the nitty-gritty of human temptations and all the nooks and crannies of human life (Hebrews 4:15).

Jesus learned to deliberately and voluntarily accept His calling and to yield (to the extent of the cross) His life to the will and purpose of the Father. Consequently, He received the Holy Spirit's ministry in full union with His own. Simpson believed that the believer has not only the same need but the same privilege and right of a union and filling. This divine provision is perfectly natural and suited to common human need. Sanctification that is expressed as superiority or a dehumanized piety is likely a pious fraud.

Sanctification and the Parallel of Christ's Relationship to the Kingdom

When Jesus said, "If I drive out demons by the Spirit of God, then the kingdom of God has come upon you" (Matthew 12:28), He was proclaiming the new rights and privileges being opened for His disciples. By His identification with man, He opened the way for believers to have the same relationship He had with the Spirit of God. Simpson observes: "This gives perpetuity to all the supernatural features of Christ's life and work and the apostolic age and, as someone has said with great beauty and power, it makes the Lord Jesus our contemporary to the end of time."[5] Christ Himself established a continuity with us in His kingdom work through the ministry of the Holy Spirit.

The power of Christ's kingdom has never impacted the church as it should, according to Simpson, but will someday be realized. The kingdom has come in our midst:

> *The promise of the departing Master is just as true as we shall allow Him to make it. "Lo, I am with you all the days, even unto the end of the age. He that believeth in me, the works that I do shall he do also, and greater works than these shall he do because*

I go unto my Father." But when this fully dawns upon the con-
ception of the church of God, she will arise to her heavenly
birthright, and the promise of Joel will be fulfilled in a more glo-
rious way than has been witnessed even in the past. "I will
show signs and wonders in heaven above and in the earth
beneath before the coming of the great and notable day of the
Lord." [6]

Simpson's concept of sanctification was not limited to a
life of victory over sin and self, or even to power for service. He
saw a life in such union with Christ that the same sovereign will
and power of the Spirit demonstrated in Christ will now work
dynamically in and through sanctified believers. The result,
however, will be greater because Jesus has been glorified and
the church has been instituted to respond to her heavenly
birthright!

Jesus' proclamation that the kingdom had come nigh for
His followers was fulfillment pictured in the Old Testament by
the year of Jubilee: "Someone has well called it the Gospel of
Jubilee, for the whole setting of the proclamation is just a
figure and the frame of Israel's year of Jubilee."[7] One of these
days, in Simpson's thought, the church will awaken to her
heavenly birthright and the promise of Joel will come to pass
in a more glorious fulfillment.

In this context of Christ's kingdom sanctification has its
brightest and fullest meaning. Without this framework personal
sanctification tends to become narrow and isolated.[8] Sanctification has an ultimate purpose higher than the mere cor-
recting of personal deficiencies caused by sin. Ephesians 5:25
asserts that Christ gave Himself up for the church to make her
holy, and the same epistle teaches that "God placed all things
under [Christ's] feet and appointed him to be head over
everything for the church, which is his body, the fullness of him
who fills everything in every way" (Ephesians 1:22-23).

The fullness of Christ relates both to the church and creation itself since "He fills everything in every way." Even as is true of Christ, sanctified believers live sacrificially for the church to be completed and for Christ to come again so that the kingdom may be established. This will unite heaven and earth in the fullness of Christ. The fullness of Christ and the fullness of the Spirit are integral to the kingdom Christ came to establish. Simpson envisioned the practical relevance of this:

> *This same mighty power is as necessary today in the perfection of ecclesiastical machinery. We are in danger of forgetting it. Modern schools, medical missions, industrial teaching, and a thousand other things can never take the place of the baptism of the Holy Ghost. The fullness of this power will never be known except in connection with the world's evangelization. It is for this that Christ especially promised it. As we seek it, that we may be witnesses unto Him, we may claim it without limitation, and the wider our witness-bearing, the more glorious the power will be.*[9]

Sanctification and the Parallel of Personal and Corporate Expression

One of the more lucid, theological writings of Alliance tradition came from W.C. Stevens in his book *The Triumphs of the Cross.*[10] As a life-long worker in the C&MA and principal of The Missionary Training Institute during most years that Simpson led the Alliance, he reflected the significance which the doctrine of sanctification held in the C&MA. The contents of Stevens' book were initially presented to "a little company of God's children assembled for seven days in August, 1903." In order, as the invitation read, "to enjoy unhurried, unhindered seasons of prayer together as fellow-members of the Body of Christ, and to learn at the feet of the Lord Jesus Christ some deeper lessons of the cross of Calvary."[11]

Stevens' vision of the atonement governed his vision of

the sanctified life. Charles Blanchard, president of Wheaton College, wrote a foreword for a new edition in 1915 and said: "In this day when so many pass the cross and look upon it as a needless thing, those who realize as Mr. Stevens does, that it is everything to the needy souls of men, have a right to speak."[12] Stevens treats 10 great relations between the cross of Jesus Christ and redemption: the cross as related to the Mosaic law, to regeneration, to the world, to Satan, to sickness, to cleansing, to the "old man," to suffering, to the church and to a perishing world. Thus, the cross was the negotiating basis for every grace and blessing offered by heaven to meet human need.

As Jesus anticipated Calvary, He made this assertion in His high-priestly prayer: "For them I sanctify myself, that they too may be truly sanctified" (John 17:19). Suffering is commonly associated with physical or emotional pain, but suffering for Jesus was a matter of being willing to be a sanctified offering for the needs of others—the needs of His disciples and the needs of the world.

The birth of Christ was the beginning of this offering, but the offering was not complete until a life of obedient submission to God was fulfilled in human life. Only then was it given as a sanctified offering on Calvary. The physical was coincidental to the sanctification experienced by Christ, but it was an important element to the whole person of Christ (as directly implied in Romans 12:1-2).

The cross in penal satisfaction is also to be the cross in believers, says Stevens.[13] The cross of Jesus is to become the believer's cross in identification with Christ's ministry for bringing in the kingdom.

This really is what sanctification is all about. To narrow the meaning to a life of victory or to power for service or to a life of blessing is inadequate and tends to be misleading. It is the all-sufficiency of Christ for total humanness as negotiated by the cross and lived out in ministry for the world and the kingdom.

Jesus said, "Anyone who loves his father or mother more than me is not worthy of me; anyone who loves his son or daughter more than me is not worthy of me; and anyone who does not take his cross and follow me is not worthy of me. Whoever finds his life will lose it, and whoever loses his life for my sake will find it" (Matthew 10:37-39). To be worthy of Christ's fellowship in life and ministry with the authority and power His Spirit provides, believers must identify with the cross. This is transforming and becomes an ongoing experience expressed in our love for Christ in corporate ministry.

Identification with the cross is no casual affair incidentally associated with regeneration. It is part of the full salvation God has provided by making Christ our Sanctifier as well as Savior. A process is involved, which Stevens explains in this way:

> *God does not sanction the continuance of sin at all, either in the sense of outward acts or of inward spirit. He demands the surrender of sinful acts and sinful will for immediate, full cleansing by the blood. Thus the heart is made pure for the indwelling of Christ. But there remains the great experience of "growing up into Him in all things," the assimilation, we might express it, of every part of our natures to His likeness. He takes time in this work of reconstruction, and for the time being He satisfies Himself with conditions which in due season He means to supersede.*
>
> *There is a sense in which the old man in this last meaning is instantaneously put off. Just as the "Old South" one day, after having laid down the arms of succession, submitted herself to be reconstructed, so the soul, after laying down active warfare against God and the principle of sin as well, is called to submit itself for entire reconstruction. But submission to reconstruction had to be practiced by the South through many a hard testing, and that principle of submission is having to be acted upon still today for much unfinished work of reconstruction, and few of us, to say the least, are yet through with this putting off. But the old*

> *man in this sense should never be confounded with sin, neither should God's moving upon nature with transforming opera tion be regarded by us as being a condemning of sin on His part.*[14]

Simpson's approach is very similar. He illustrates sanctification as a process with the analogy of tenement buildings and miserable shanties on valuable property in New York City. As any purchaser would have no interest in patching and repairing the worthless buildings, so also Christ has no interest in repairing our lives:

> *All I want is the ground, the site, and when I get it I will raze the old heap of rubbish to the foundations, and dig deep down to the solid rock before I build my splendid mansion. . . . I do not want a vestige of your house, all that I require is the situation.*[15]

God wants to use the possibilities of our lives for a temple structure that "looks out upon eternity and commands a view of all that is glorious in the possibilities of existence. . . . He is the Author and Finisher of our faith, and the true attitude of the consecrated heart is that of a constant yielding and constant receiving. This last view of sanctification gives a boundless scope to our spiritual progress. It is here that the gradual phase of sanctification comes in."[16]

To interpret these illustrations is to understand that Jesus Christ, the sinless One, bore our sin by identification (not sympathy): "He was made to be sin for us." The sin Jesus bore was our radical independence from God as inherited from Adam. This could only be removed by the Second Adam. Fleshly sins result from claiming my right to myself, which is really a pseudo claim if Jesus is our Lord and Savior. The ground has been purchased, but submission to reconstruction is necessary. The pseudo claim of maintaining the old shanty must be acknowledged and confessed if our identification and union with Christ is to result in progressive sanctification.

The natural is not sinful, but the things that often seem right and noble in the natural keep us from God's best. They are the daubing and fixing of the old shanty. Deliverance from sin is not deliverance from human nature. The total human nature is the site Jesus purchased. We are justified and made new creations by an imputed righteousness. But through Jesus as our Sanctifier, the very nature of Jesus is imparted to us, transforming our human nature. As we abide in Him, Jesus' nature becomes transfused with our nature and God's own reconstruction of our human nature becomes progressive.

Union with Christ will bring us under the same kind of testing, temptation and responsibility Jesus bore. Faith brings us into a living relationship with Christ, and through suffering we gain new capacity to experience the fullness and beauty of Christ. To know Christ as Sanctifier is to be a part of the fellowship of Christ's suffering and this becomes foundational to any corporate ministry.

Again, sanctification goes beyond any concept of holiness equated with sinless perfection or suppressionism. In fact, if Christ is our righteousness and we fully abide in Him and the cross, we seek no perfection of our own but only Christ Himself. As sanctified believers we are not to be introverted over the sin question or concerns about inbred sin. Our preoccupation is to be with Christ and His full salvation. Neither are we to be obsessed with the Holy Spirit and the gifts of the Spirit. Rather, we receive, cultivate and honor the Holy Spirit to reveal Christ and His fullness for the gifts He wishes to manifest in the body of Christ. This is how progression in sanctification will find its fullest expression.

What is experienced in personal sanctification also is to be manifest in the corporate life of the church. As Ephesians observes: "Christ loved the church and gave himself up for her to make her holy, cleansing her by the washing with water through the word, and to present her to himself as a radiant church, without stain or wrinkle or any other blemish, but holy and blameless" (Ephesians 5:25-27). The church is a special object for the sanctifying work of Jesus Christ. This is reflected in Paul's epistles to the churches of Rome, Corinth, Ephesus and Colosse.

There is no doubt, that progression in sanctification was Paul's chief concern for the churches he ministered to and it is Christ's primary concern. Out of sanctification emerges deeper worship, richer fellowship, fuller equipping in nurture and training, a more effective evangelism and power in missions.

Sanctification is not intended for isolated individuals but for the building, equipping, beautifying and enabling of the church in its life and ministry. Stevens observes: "Christ our Lord incorporates into a body all whom He saves individually; and so He stands as head and Savior to the whole body, and as such to us individually in, not separate from, that body."[17] It is in this regard that Christ's love for the body, the church, and His ministry to it, is to be revealed in us. The Scriptures teach that believers are members of His body, of His flesh and His bones, and Stevens adds, "This does not mean His body in heaven but the church, His body on earth. His body on earth is made up of people in flesh and bones, and we are members of His earthly flesh-and-bones body."[18]

Progressive sanctification in the corporate body has a contagious effect and healing virtue. This is illustrated by Stevens by the analogy of the human body: "Just as our heart, in sending forth the life-blood throughout the entire body, places each member under the law of the heart to pass on to its fellow member, until the whole circuit is completed and the blood returns to the heart; even so Christ, in sending forth His love by the Spirit through the whole church, places each member under His own law of love. Only in fulfilling that law do we send back to Him after full circulation His own current of love

and have it maintained fresh and strong for ourselves."[19]
Stevens' ecclesiology usually focused the "wholeness" of
the church to a transdenominational vision. Nevertheless,
the implication drawn is that corporate sanctification is Christ's
own heart and life-blood pulsating through the body, giving
energy, healing and life to the whole. It is in relationship to the
body that individual members will more fully experience progressive sanctification in its intended working and where participation in the extension of the kingdom can find its highest
expression.

In Ephesians 5:25-27, where Christ is said to have given
Himself to the church ". . . that he might sanctify and cleanse
it with the washing of the water by the word" (KJV), Stevens
interprets the meaning as the cleansing of the way, the nature,
the old creation. He writes:

> *It is the Potter dashing in the water from time to time and work-*
> *ing it through. . . . That is more than purification by the blood*
> *from all sin; and it is not right to say that that which is to be puri-*
> *fied into His very likeness is sinful. "Seeing ye have purified your*
> *souls in obeying the truth through the Spirit unto unfeigned love*
> *of the brethren, see that ye love one another with a pure heart fer-*
> *vently" (I Peter 1:22). Love of the brethren begins with regener-*
> *ation; it is made purer in sanctification. But, either very few are*
> *sanctified, or there is some further purifying needed to bring*
> *about the brotherly love which the Spirit within us bears witness*
> *we ought to have in full union with Jesus Christ. This is brought*
> *about, not by instantaneous cleansing from sin by the blood, but*
> *"in obeying the truth through the Spirit," that is, the Potter*
> *dashing in more water and working it through.*[20]

The parallelisms Jesus drew of His relationship to the Father
to the believer's relationship with Him in love, unity, truth,
glory and sentness in His high-priestly prayer, are virtues God
wants perfected in the body of Christ. These are virtues to
which Jesus was sanctified in His Father during His earthly life

and to which believers are to be sanctified in Christ. This sanctification comes by "obeying the truth through the Spirit" and is not instantaneous. Immature leaders will not produce mature churches. To have the water of the Word worked through the body in wise application is one of the greatest needs of the church today. God has chosen the church to extend His kingdom but the molding, fitting and sanctifying of His church for kingdom work is crucial to everything the church does.

Sanctification and the Parallel of Doctrinal and Practical Expression

The practical outworking of the doctrine of sanctification in personal lives and in the corporate life of believers has many ramifications. But ultimately, sanctification is the shaping of lives for eternity and the perfecting of His body, the church, for the fulfillment of Christ's kingdom and the coming of our Lord. Simpson wrote:

> *The hope of the church and the Christian is the coming of our Lord and Savior Jesus Christ and the kingdom which He is to set upon this blighted and misgoverned world. He has told us that His kingdom is not of this world. It has a spiritual form in the present age consisting of all those who are quickened and united with Himself by the Holy Ghost. But the manifestation of the kingdom is reserved for His glorious appearing as King of kings and Lord of Lords.*[21]

It is in the light of eternity that the present becomes most significant. If the incarnational life of Christ on earth and the giving of that life on Calvary is the fulcrum of all divine revelation to man, and if man created in God's image is to be redemptively restored from the fall to the image of Christ, then sanctification is basic to all that human living, the church's ministry and the kingdom are about. For this reason sanctification was basic to world missions in the mind of Simpson. It is not an additive or expediency for the task of missions, but the foundational ground for life and service both for the individual believer and for the church. Christ Himself is to be incarnated in believers personally and in the church corporately for an effective worldwide witness that Christ's kingdom may come.

However, both Simpson's and Stevens' ecclesiology was focused on the church transdenominationally; the C&MA was conceived as para-denominational and not as para-church.[22] The significance, discipline and accountability of the local church from its initial planting to its full stature in Christ was not emphasized because the Alliance was not a church. The idealisms of a transdenominational church expressed in their ecclesiology fitted the nature of the C&MA as a society, but must now be translated as a church and as a denomination.

That the church is incarnational in nature is clear both in Simpson and Stevens, but ecclesiology was glossed and idealized in evangelicalism and etherealized by dispensational-fundamentalism in the late 19th and early 20th century. It was not until the indigenous nature of the church became an urgent necessity in the 1950s, followed by the church-growth movement, that a more adequate and practical understanding of ecclesiology came into significant focus for the C&MA. Nevertheless, the idealisms early Alliance leaders attached to sanctification in the evangelical church are vitally relevant for the local church today.

Stevens provides various practical insights into the working of progressive sanctification in corporate and personal faith expression.

(1) *Love of the brethren is made purer by sanctification.* This body-life result is contingent on a purifying that comes by "obeying the truth through the Spirit" (1 Peter 1:22), as noted above. God is seeking to sanctify and cleanse the church "by

the washing with water through the word" (Ephesians 5:25). Entire consecration is followed by a discipline of progressive sanctification that is not an instantaneous cure-all, but a submissive responsiveness to God's Word and Spirit that brings about purer love. Thus, sanctification is seen as a gradual transformation of what Stevens calls "creaturely affections and desires."

It is of interest in this connection, that Jesus' prayer in John 17 was that believers might be sanctified through the truth and "be brought to complete unity to let the world know that you sent me and have loved them even as you have loved me" (verse 23). The interrelation Jesus expressed between truth, love, unity and world evangelism was associated with a sanctification in which He was in believers and believers in Him, just as the Father was in Him and He was in the Father. This was not a mere idealism but something believers needed to be brought into by "sanctification through the truth." It is not an aside from the cross but the anticipated result of it.

(2) *Disciplinary providence is made profitable through sanctification by the Word.* Stevens writes:

> *There is another great factor in this work of changing us from the old man into the new by the Word, and that is disciplinary providence. This is the strong hand of the Potter kneading the clay in conjunction with the water of the Word. The great proof-passage on this point is Heb. xii. 5-11. This "chastening" is "for our profit, that we might be partakers of His holiness"; and "it yieldeth the peaceable fruit of righteousness unto them which are exercised thereby." Holiness is more than freedom from sin. In some sense, holiness is instantly obtained; in another sense, it is a matter of time and discipline, dependent upon the Potter's wise application of the Word under testing and chastening providences. What a difference there is in the quality of holiness in a newly sanctified person and in a deeply chastened spirit! What a*

*difference there is between a newly surrendered will and a thor-
oughly disciplined will!"*[23]

Paul's consternation over the foolishness of the Galatians,
who were so easily moved from the gospel, caused him to tra-
vail for them until Christ was formed in them (Galatians
4:19). It was not that the Galatians were not believers, but
they were immature and ungrounded through the sanctification of the Word. Stevens observes that lack of understanding
this aspect of sanctification causes painful perplexity, needless
self-condemnation and anxiety by directly associating this
with sin and failure. God's chastening in providence should not
be seen as punishment for sin, but as corrections of our earthly natures and working out the new creation to completion.
"He can give no time-allowance to sin, but He can to this
renewing of nature. Hence we need to stand with God in this
work in a right attitude."[24]

Several guidelines are suggested by Stevens to prevent perplexity and anxiety:

(a) Rest in God's hands trustfully and peacefully. *Rest-
lessness, doubt and worry become a hindrance. "God could
instantly annihilate the flesh of the old creation. But that is not
His pleasure. He is pleased not to destroy one atom of this lump
of potter's clay, but to reconstitute every atom of it into Christ-
likeness. Many are trying to get God to electrocute their natures.
This is folly. God will not destroy His own creation, but will lift
it into a higher order. Rest in the steady exercises of faith, love and
praise through the Holy Spirit, who has come and who abides in
transforming power and working."*[25]

(b) Realize that the Word is most needed when we
are going through renewing processes in providential
testing. *Man is not to live by bread alone but by every word that
proceeds from the mouth of God. The Word is for correction, for
instruction in righteousness that the man of God may be perfect
and furnished for every good work (paraphrased from Matthew*

4:4 and 2 Timothy 3:16-17).

(c) Enjoy God in present providence. *"It may be in being wronged, persecuted, oppressed, baffled, perplexed; nevertheless, it is God's providence, belonging to the 'all things' which work together for good.* . . . *And even the deep sense of the elements of the old creation yet remaining in us is not to disturb our tranquil enjoyment of God; for what He for the time tranquilly allows we must also thus bear with in ourselves."* [26]

Joy in suffering is not a pleasure found in being abused or dominated by evil, but the finding of new capacity by the Holy Spirit to overcome evil through our union with Jesus Christ. Thus the power, authority and presence of Jesus will become more manifest and enjoyed in present providence.

(3) *The cross will sanctify the Body of Christ for greater effectiveness in a perishing world.* Christ laying down His life for the church should result in believers being self-sacrificing to minister to the needs and shortcomings of the church. This, says Stevens, is not possible by our own resources: "If Christ had only laid down His life in death for us and did not impart His nature to us through the Spirit, it would be useless for us to try to fulfil the obligation to imitate His example of love. But the 'ought' springs altogether as a possibility from the fact that He laid down His life to give it to us in the Spirit, so that our obligation carries ability with it."[27]

The cross will sanctify our gifts of ministry for mutual edification. Christ as living Head has sent the Holy Spirit to administer gifts to represent Him in the variety distributed. Discouragement is avoided because our individual gifts are tempered for the whole body; pride is avoided because the gift of each member needs the gift-ministry of others to represent the whole. But it is in and through the cross that these relationships are sanctified.

It is by the sanctification of the cross that the assembling of believers is maintained in togetherness. "We are liable to impulses in determining our associations, which would dry up love and paralyze good works; and we need to make special room for the spirit of the cross in us to turn an occasion for separation into one for closer, stronger, truer fellowship."[28] Peace and forgiveness come by the cross in order that service by love may become more effective in reaching the world for Christ. The sanctifying spirit of the cross is central to the body-life of the church as God's ordained agency to reach the world for Christ.

The Parallel of Faith and Holiness

"The reason that a great many Christians have so little faith is because they are living in the world and in themselves, and separated in so large a part of their life from God and holiness. . . . faith requires for its heavenly vision the highlands of holiness and separation, and the clear, pure sky of a consecrated life," wrote Simpson.[29]

Faith is simply our capacity to receive Christ, "a shell to hold His fullness." Too often the shell is shrunk and shriveled by sin and doubt, reliance on human wisdom, by self-sufficiency and dependence on our strength, by reliance on external evidences, and fruitless struggle to work up faith. But the soul that knows Christ's fullness in sanctifying grace, has unlimited possibilities of faith because of fresh and new capacity to know Christ. Thus faith enlarges with progressive sanctification which Simpson calls "the larger Christian life" (as an expression in Second Corinthians 6:13 (KJV)—"Be ye also enlarged").

Progressive sanctification and an enlarged faith charged all of Simpson's motivations. In *A Larger Christian Life*, a glimpse of this is caught in this summarization of what God's people need:[30]

(1) Believers need a larger vision of who Jesus is in truth. What He should mean to our generation for life and work. His commands and promises are presently relevant. Our eyes need enlightenment regarding the hope of His calling and what our inheritance in Christ represents.

(2) Believers need a larger faith that will appropriate the promises and will rise to the level of every emergency we meet. They need a measure of light and power that can grasp the victory God desires to give.

(3) Believers need a larger love that will love others as Christ loves us. They need a love that will love the lost and delight to suffer and sacrifice for their salvation. A love that will take a brother's need and pain as though it were our own.

(4) Believers need a larger joy that delights in God Himself and His power and goodness. Such joy will overcome darkness and apparent desertion with faith and perseverance that establishes character. Simpson says: "We need a joy so large, so deep, so divine that it will not feel its sacrifices, will not talk about its trials, but will 'endure the cross despising the shame,' 'for the joy set before us'."[31]

(5) Believers need a larger experience with a range of Christian living that can bring Christ into every situation and prove His faithfulness.

(6) Believers need a larger sphere of service that is creative in the unfamiliar areas of need. The unexpected can be met in a spiritual stride that opens new opportunities for witness. In particular callings believers are to recognize ways to extend "the testimony of Jesus in all His fullness to all the world."

(7) Believers need a larger hope that vividly, personally, definitely anticipates the Lord's coming. The inspiring, stimulating and quickening motive this provides is to be intensified.

(8) Believers also need a larger baptism of the Spirit: "We need more room for His indwelling, more scope for His expanding, more channels for His outflow."[32]

The expansive outlook Simpson had for the enlarging of faith and for progressive sanctification of believers personally and corporately was like the blending of earth and sky in glorious sunrise. The possibilities for faith are limitless in progressive sanctification but there is a relational interdependence on which such progression depends. This interdependence is true whether believers are conscious of it or not. Every phase of progression is dependent on the whole and a biblical and intelligent vision for divine sanctification should govern and charge every motivation and activity of the believer and of the church.

FOOTNOTES

[1] Paraphrased from *The Higher Christian Life* by A. B. Simpson, p. 42.

[2] A.B. Simpson, "The Holy Spirit and the Gospel," (Gospel Tabernacle Pulpit, Weekly Sermon) *The Christian and Missionary Alliance*, March 4, 1905, p. 133.

[3] Ibid.

[4] Ibid., p. 134.

[5] Ibid.

[6] Ibid.

[7] Ibid.

[8] Oswald Chambers observed: "The Higher Christian Life movements tend to develop along the lines of spiritual isolation." Mrs. Oswald Chambers, *Oswald Chambers—His Life and Work*, (London: Simpkin Marshall Ltd., 1933), p. 331. Boardman mostly individualized the higher life, as did Hannah Whitall Smith in *The Christian's Secret of a Happy Life*, representative of this movement.

[9] A.B. Simpson, *Missionary Messages*, p. 27.

[10] W.C. Stevens, *The Triumphs of the Cross*, (San Francisco: McClinton & Co., 1915), Reprint. As a graduate of Union Seminary with a doctorate from a university in Germany and fluent in six languages, Stevens was a thorough student

but shunned academic notoriety.

[11] Ibid., "Prefatory Notes" by Max Wood Moorhead, p. 3.

[12] Ibid., "Prefatory Notes" by Charles A. Blanchard.

[13] Ibid., p. 63.

[14] Ibid., p. 53.

[15] A.B. Simpson, *Wholly Sanctified*, p. 22.

[16] Ibid., p. 23.

[17] Stevens, *The Triumphs of the Cross*, p. 69.

[18] Ibid., pp. 69-70.

[19] Ibid., p. 71.

[20] Ibid., p. 55.

[21] A.B. Simpson, *The Old Faith and the New Gospel*, (Harrisburg: Christian Publications, Inc., 1966), Reprint, p. 68.

[22] That the C&MA was para-denominational and not para-church may seem insignificant, but it reflects an ecclesiology that accepts local evangelical churches as responsible representations of a larger body. The Alliance branch members were encouraged to be responsible members in existing churches. After The Christian Alliance and The Evangelical Missionary Alliance joined in 1897, an annual Council was devised to involve a responsible constituency in policy and leadership direction. Though fund-raising was an important part of missionary conventions, it was not its primary purpose. This ministry was to introduce believers to the deeper life and to inspire branch members to faith in an all-sufficient Christ. Extensive preaching preceded the missionary emphasis.

The missionary convention was also a report system of divine working with praise and thanksgiving and the raising of prayer warriors to intercede for needs. Also, it was an important means for missionary recruitment. Annual missionary pledges were viewed not merely as funding devises but rather as consistent expressions of vital and total support.

Simpson deplored in publication the proliferation of

independent missionary agencies or para-church organizations because they lacked a responsible constituency and their leadership practiced a shallow accountability in doctrine, discipline and direction. Though he praised their fellowship in the gospel he viewed them as sub-biblical in operation.

[23] Stevens, *The Triumphs of the Cross,* p. 56.

[24] Ibid., p. 57.

[25] Ibid.

[26] Ibid., pp. 57-58

[27] Ibid., p. 71.

[28] Ibid., p. 75

[29] Simpson, *A Larger Christian Life,* p. 58.

[30] Ibid., pp. 53-59.

[31] Ibid., p. 56.

[32] Ibid., p. 57.

The following books which were used as sources in *Sancti-fication: An Alliance Distinctive* are still readily available. You may purchase them through your local Christian bookstore, or by calling Christian Publications, toll-free, 1-800-233-4443.

Books by Dr. A.B. Simpson

The Cross of Christ
The Fourfold Gospel
Himself
The Holy Spirit, Vol. 1
The Holy Spirit, Vol. 2
A Larger Christian Life
Missionary Messages
When the Comforter Came
Wholly Sanctified

Other books cited:

George Pardington
The Crisis of the Deeper Life
Outline Studies in Christian Doctrine

Robert Nicklaus, John Sawin, Samuel Stoesz
All for Jesus

A.E. Thompson
A.B. Simpson, His Life and Work

A.W. Tozer
Wingspread: A.B. Simpson—A Study in Spiritual Altitude